Breakfast
for the SOUL

Compiled by Judith Couchman

RIVER
OAK
PUBLISHING

Tulsa, Oklahoma

Breakfast for the Soul
ISBN 1-58919-994-4
Copyright © 1998, 2001 by Judy C. Couchman

Published by RiverOak Publishing
P.O. Box 700143
Tulsa, Oklahoma 74170-0143

Published in association with the literary agency of Alive Communication, Inc., 1465 Kelly Johnson Blvd., Suite 320, Colorado Springs, CO 80920.

For my nephews:
Brian, Andy, Tony

May your souls grow heartily.

Acknowledgments

Thanks to RiverOak Publishing and other publishers for the privilege of compiling and publishing the works of committed and inspiring Christians, past and present. And to Rebecca Currington, editor, for her support and enthusiasm.

Thanks, too, to my prayer team—Charette Barta, Win Couchman, Madalene Harris, Karen Hilt, and Nancy Lemons—for their prayers for this project. We hope that you'll be refreshed and nourished each day by *Breakfast for the Soul.*

Introduction

"Eat your breakfast. It's the most important meal of the day."

Growing up, we heard this message, and its common sense about "starting the day right" will follow us for a lifetime.

Good advice is like that. It "sticks to the ribs" of the soul and reminds us to live well and wisely. Accordingly, wisdom teaches us that robust living depends on healthy nourishment in the morning, both physical and spiritual.

Through the ages, well-known and everyday Christians have talked about meeting God in the morning, to feed their souls, offer petitions, and glean insights for the day. The psalmist wrote, "In the morning, O LORD, you hear my voice; in the morning I lay my requests before you and wait in expectation" (Psalm 5:3 NIV). John Bunyan wrote, "He who runs from God in the morning will scarcely find Him the rest of the day." Corrie ten Boom considered morning "quiet time" with God "the key for the day." There is something about meeting God in the morning—even if your morning begins later than most—that points an anxious heart and mind in His peaceable direction.

Meeting God in the morning—eating a spiritual breakfast—usually means taking time for Scripture and prayer, but it's also helpful to gather wisdom from mature Christians through devotional or meditative readings. And that's the purpose of this book. Its pages are filled with hope, advice, inspiration, and encouragement from believers, past and present, who've consistently walked with God.

As you consider their thoughts, you'll discover that frequently a selected reading will focus on your precise need for that day—for this is how God works. If we are faithful to turn our thoughts toward Him, He'll meet us at our point of need, refreshing and encouraging us with His truth and presence.

However you choose to use this book, whatever your need, with the help of devoted believers, you can start each day with spiritual meaning, knowing you've fed yourself with *Breakfast for the Soul*.

Judy Couchman

Contents

Our Good God

God is great, and therefore He will be sought;
He is good, and therefore He will be found.

—Anonymous

1

In the Beginning

John R. W. Stott

The Gospel does not consist of what we can do for ourselves,
but of what God stands ready to do for us.

—*Arkansas Methodist*

"In the beginning God." The first four words of the Bible are more than an introduction to the creation story or to the book of Genesis. They supply the key which opens our understanding of the Bible as a whole. They tell us that the religion of the Bible is a religion of the initiative of God.

You can never take God by surprise. You can never anticipate Him. He always makes the first move. He is always there "in the beginning." Before man existed, God acted. Before man stirs himself to seek God, God has sought man. In the Bible, we do not see man groping after God; we see God reaching after man.

Many people visualize a God Who sits comfortably on a distant throne, remote, aloof, uninterested, and indifferent to the need of mortals, until, it may be, they can badger Him into taking action on their behalf. Such a view is wholly false. The Bible reveals a God who, long before it even occurs to man to turn to Him, while man is still lost in darkness and sunk in sin, takes the initiative, rises from His throne, lays aside His glory, and stoops to seek until He finds him.

This sovereign, anticipating activity of God is seen in many ways.

He has taken the initiative in creation, bringing the universe and its contents into existence: "In the beginning God created the heavens and the earth" (Genesis 1:1 NIV).

He has taken the initiative in revelation, making known to mankind both His nature and His will: "In many and various ways God spoke of old to our fathers by the prophets; but in these last days he has spoken to us by a Son. He has taken the initiative in salvation, coming in Jesus Christ to set men and women free from their sins: God has visited and redeemed His people" (Hebrews 1:1-2).

God has created. God has spoken. God has acted. These statements of God's initiative in three different spheres form a summary of the religion of the Bible. God has spoken and acted in Jesus Christ. He has said something. He has done something.

It is neither a collection of religious ideas nor a catalog of rules. It is a "gospel"—the good news. In Paul's words, it is "the gospel of God . . . concerning His Son Jesus Christ our Lord" (Romans 1:1,3). It is not primarily an invitation to man to do anything; it is supremely a declaration of what God has done in Christ for human beings like ourselves. ✿

But God demonstrates his own love for us in this:
While we were still sinners, Christ died for us.

—Romans 5:8 NIV

✿

We can learn nothing of the gospel except by feeling its truths.
There are some sciences that may be learned by the head,
but the science of Christ crucified can only
be learned by the heart.

—Charles Haddon Spurgeon

2
God Is Easy to Live With

A. W. Tozer

*The very word "God" suggests care, kindness, goodness; and
the idea of God in His infinity is infinite care, infinite kindness, infinite goodness.
We give God the name of good;
it is only by shortening it that it becomes God.*

—Henry Ward Beecher

It is most important to our spiritual welfare that we hold in our minds a right conception of God. If we think of Him as cold and exacting, we shall find it impossible to love Him, and our lives will be ridden with servile fear. If again, we hold Him to be kind and understanding, our whole inner life will mirror that idea.

The truth is that God is the most winsome of all beings and His service one of unspeakable pleasure. He is all love, and those who trust Him need never know anything but that love. He is just, indeed, and He will not condone sin; but through the blood of the everlasting covenant He is able to act toward us exactly as if we had never sinned. Toward the trusting sons of men His mercy will always triumph over justice.

The fellowship of God is delightful beyond all telling. He communes with His redeemed ones in an easy, uninhibited fellowship that is restful and healing to the soul. He is not sensitive or selfish or temperamental. What He is today we shall find Him tomorrow and the next day and the next year. He is quick to overlook imperfections when He knows we meant to do His will. He loves us for ourselves and values our love more than galaxies of new created worlds.

How good it would be if we could learn that God is easy to live with. He remembers our frame and knows that we are dust. He may sometimes chasten us, it is true, but even this He does with a smile, the proud, tender smile of a Father Who is bursting with pleasure over an imperfect but promising son who is coming every day to look more and more like the One Whose child he is.

Some of us are religiously jumpy and self-conscious because we know that God sees our every thought and is acquainted with all our ways. We need not be. God is the sum of all patience and the essence of kindly good will. We please Him most, not by frantically trying to make ourselves good, but by throwing ourselves into His arms with all our imperfections, and believing that He understands everything and loves us still. ❧

So we know and rely on the love God has for us. God is love. Whoever lives in love lives in God, and God in him.

—1 John 4:16 NIV

❧

*The world appears very little to a soul
that contemplates the greatness of God.
My business is to remain in the presence of God.*

— Brother Lawrence

3

In the Right Hands

Phillip Keller

He can see me—right there in His hand!

—Mother Teresa

[We cannot] be set free, unshackled, loosed except by the loving, caring, understanding hands of the Good Shepherd. [Yet] we resist His very approach. We resent His calling to us. We recoil in fear and apprehension from His overtures and good will.

Deep within us doubts and misgivings surge through our minds and emotions. Our spirits shrivel up within us. We cringe from His coming. We feel so threatened. Our wills are set in stern resistance. We are convinced we will only suffer abuse at His hands.

But it is only the hand of God that sets us free.

It is His strong hands that can turn us around and train us to move in new ways, new directions.

It is His gentle, yet strong hands, His understanding hands, which can handle us with skill and love and strength.

It is His hands which change our character, alter our conduct and send us out to do great and noble service in society.

Few of us, who have not yet come into Christ's care, think seriously enough about the sinister and subversive character of Satan. In fact, to many people he is almost less than real. He is sometimes supposed to be nothing more than a superstitious phantom, more or less the mere product of man's imagination.

The terrible truth is he is very real, very active and exceedingly deceptive. While appearing to give us liberty by allowing us to do whatever we wish in response to our own inherent selfishness or sin, he watches us actually enslave and destroy ourselves.

Many of us have been under the wrong management most of our lives. We have been in the wrong hands. We have been so mishandled that all of the original, superb purposes for which we were created have been totally distorted and misspent. We are virtual slaves to sin, to ourselves and to Satan.

Yet the Stranger of Galilee comes into our lives. He looks upon us with love. He touches us with tenderness. He sees beyond our sins. He extends His knowing hands to take us into His understanding care.

We are not always keen to go.

We are afraid He may have sinister motives.

We recoil from His control.

Life under the old master has made us very suspicious. We are not at all sure things will be any better now.

In our human ignorance and suspicion, we are convinced that to come to Christ's care can be even worse bondage than before.

It takes some of us a lifetime to learn that Christ, our Good Shepherd, knows exactly what He is doing with us. He understands us perfectly. &

The righteous and the wise and what they do are in God's hands.

—Ecclesiastes 9:1 NIV

&

We are in God's hand . . . not in theirs.

—William Shakespeare

4

A Simple, Loving Reality

Judith Couchman

Thou hast made us for Thyself, and the heart
of man is restless until it finds its rest in Thee.

— Saint Augustine

My mother still beams when she repeats this story from my oldest sister's childhood. It varies a bit with each telling, but the message remains constant. Whenever Shirley would return home from kindergarten or any other outing without Mom, she would march into the house and yell, "I'm here!" This announcement would signal my mother's part in the routine: she fawned over her daughter's presence.

Mom had no trouble with her role in the performance. This young child issued from her blood; this Shirley Temple look-alike sprang from her loving procreation. How could she not delight in her daughter's existence? Any other response would have been utterly unthinkable. Nearly fifty years later, Mother still feels this joy in regard to her children and grandchildren. Though she encourages and revels in our accomplishments, more than anything Mom loves us just because we belong to her.

This, too, is the way of God the Father. He declares to His children, "I have loved you with an everlasting love." He draws us to Himself for the sheer pleasure of it. He loves us not for who we are, or what we do, or who we can or will be. He loves us because He created us, because we belong to Him.

It is a profoundly simple reality.

A beautiful work of art sits in my upstairs bedroom, the kind that beckons attention, evokes emotion, and lingers in the mind. It is an exquisite piece of pottery that woos and teases passersby. Half vase because of its small pedestal bottom and half pot due to its wide girth and mouth, this creation embodies the word *unique*. I would admire this intriguing artwork no matter what, but it's especially meaningful because my friend Pat thoughtfully shaped the piece and presented it to me as a birthday gift. It serves as a monument to our friendship.

A narrow-eyed pragmatist might examine this creation and announce, "What good is it? It doesn't do anything." And yes, I could fill the pot with pine cones or tennis balls or jewelry or whatever—just to assign it something to do—but that would detract from its intrinsic beauty. All things considered, I value the pottery's form more than its function.

This is how God feels about us. We are His beautiful and thoughtful creation. Like one-of-a-kind pottery, above all else He treasures our innate worth. We are immensely significant, and our value does not depend on anything we do, think, say, feel, earn, inherit or look like. It is because we exist as God's creation. *Finis*. Nothing more. ॐ

I have loved you with an everlasting love;
therefore I have continued my faithfulness to you.

—Jeremiah 31:3 RSV

It was for love that God created the world.
It was for love that God made man in His
own image, thus making him a partner in love,
a being to whom He speaks, who He loves like a son,
and who can answer Him and love Him like a father.

—Paul Tournier

5

For Mercy's Sake

Pope John Paul II

Man may dismiss compassion from his heart, but God never will.

—William Cowper

The present-day mentality, more perhaps than that of people in the past, seems opposed to a God of mercy. In fact, it tends to exclude from life and to remove from the human heart the idea of mercy.

The word and the concept of "mercy" seem to cause uneasiness in man, who, thanks to the enormous development of science and technology never before known in history, has become the master of the earth and has subdued and dominated it. This dominion over the earth seems to leave no room for mercy.

The truth about God the "Father of Mercies" enables us to see Him as particularly close to man when he is under threat at the very heart of his existence and dignity. And this is why, in the situation of the world today, many individuals and groups guided by a lively sense of faith are turning, I would say almost spontaneously, to the mercy of God. They are certainly being moved to do this by Christ Himself, Who through His Spirit works within human hearts. Before His own townspeople in Nazareth, Christ refers to the words of the prophet Isaiah: "The Spirit of the Lord is upon me, because he has anointed me to preach the good news to the poor" (Isaiah 61:1).

Especially through His lifestyle and His actions, Jesus revealed that love is present in the world in which we live— an effective love, a love that addresses itself to man and embraces everything that makes up His humanity. This love makes itself particularly noticed in contact with human suffering, injustice and poverty—in contact with the whole historical human condition, which in various ways manifests man's limitation and frailty, both physical and moral. It is precisely the mode and sphere in which love manifests itself that in biblical language is called "mercy."

Christ reveals God as rich in mercy. The truth is not just the subject of teaching. It is the reality made present to us by Christ. Making the Father present as love and mercy is, in Christ's own consciousness, the fundamental touchstone of His mission as the Messiah.

Christ came not to condemn but to forgive, to show mercy. And the greatest mercy of all is found in His being in our midst and calling us to meet Him and to confess, with Peter, that He is the Son of the living God. No human sin can erase the mercy of God or prevent Him from unleashing all His triumphant power, if we only call upon Him. Indeed, sin itself makes even more radiant the love of the Father. In order to ransom a slave, He sacrificed His Son: His mercy toward us is redemption. ❧

For the LORD is good, his steadfast love endures for ever,
and his faithfulness to all generations.

—Psalm 100:5 RSV

❧

Among the attributes of God, although they are all equal,
mercy shines with even more brilliance than justice.

—Miguel de Cervantes

6

God's Heart-Touching Power

Frederick Buechner

Love is God's essence; power but His attribute;
therefore is His love greater than His power.

— Richard Garnett

The power of God stands in violent contrast with the power of man. It is not external like man's power, but internal. By applying external pressure, I can make a person do what I want him to do. This is man's power. But as far as making him be what I want him to be, without at the same time destroying his freedom, only love can make this happen.

And love makes it happen not coercively, but by creating a situation in which, of our own free will, we want to be what love wants us to be. And because God's love is uncoercive and treasures our freedom—if above all He wants us to love Him, then we must be left free not to love Him—we are free to resist it, deny it, crucify it finally, which we do again and again. This is our terrible freedom, which love refuses to overpower so that, in this, the greatest of all power, God's power, is itself powerless.

Maybe some say, "I know human love, and I know something of its power to heal, to set free, to give meaning and peace, but God's love I know only as a phrase." Maybe others also say this, "For all the power that human love has to heal, there is something deep within me and within the people I know best that is not healed but aches with longing still. So if God's love is powerful enough to reach that deep, how do I find it? How?"

If this is really the question, if we are really seeking this power, then I have one thing to say—perhaps it is not the only thing, but it is enormously important: ask for it. There is something in me that recoils a little at speaking so directly and childishly, but I speak this way anyway because it is the most important thing I have in me to say. Ask, and you will receive. And there is the other side to it too: If you have never known the power of God's love, then maybe it is because you have never asked to know it—I mean really asked, expecting an answer.

Seek and you will find—this power of God's love to heal, to give peace and, at least, something like real life, so that little by little, like the boy, you can get up. Yes, get up. But we must seek—like a child at first, like playing a kind of game at first because prayer is so foreign to most of us. It is so hard and it is so easy. And everything depends on it. Seek. Ask. And by God's grace we will find. ❧

Ask and it will be given to you; seek and you will find;
knock and the door will be opened to you.

—Matthew 7:7 NIV

❧

To whatever side you turn, you are forced to acknowledge
your own ignorance and the boundless power of the Creator.

—Voltaire

7

The Great Provider

Jill Briscoe

*If thou knowest God, thou knowest that
everything is possible for God to do.*

—Callimachus

God tested Abraham's faith by asking him to sacrifice his
only son, Isaac, as a burnt offering. Incredibly, Abraham set
out to do so. Taking Isaac with him to Mount Moriah, he
said to the young men, "Stay here with the donkey; the lad
and I will go yonder and worship, and we will come back to
you" (Genesis 22:5 NKJV).

Notice he said, "we will come back to you." He had faith to
believe that even if he did kill his son, God would raise him
from the dead. After all, God had told him Isaac was a very
important part of His plan of redemption for the whole world.

As Abraham raised his knife to kill Isaac, the Angel of the
Lord called to him from heaven and stopped him: "Now I
know that you fear God, seeing you have not withheld your
son, your only son, from Me" (Genesis 22:16). Abraham saw
a ram caught in the thicket and sacrificed the animal instead
of Isaac.

Because God had provided Himself a sacrifice, prefiguring
Calvary, Abraham called the name of that place *Jehovah-Jireh*,
meaning *The Lord Will Provide*. At that point, Abraham
understood a little bit more about God's redemptive character.

When Moses talked with God and asked His name, God replied, "I AM." Jehovah told Moses He had heard the people of Israel crying because of their Egyptian taskmasters, and had chosen to redeem them. "I am all that you will need as the occasion arises," He promised Moses. He is all that is needed as our occasions arise as well!

He cares when we are in bondage to some earthly taskmaster. Perhaps food or some other appetite has us whipped, and we long to be free. God has revealed Himself as our Redeemer from all bondage.

It is exactly at this point that some reject Christianity. The idea of God's relating to them in a personal way is too much for them. Somehow, the concept diminishes Him in their thinking. People feel that if God can be known, this brings Him down to their size; if He is their size, why do they need Him?

But knowing someone does not necessarily mean knowing all about them. The pot knows the feel of the Potter's hands, but because it is not the Potter, it cannot possibly fully fathom its Creator's mind. God wants us to know Him. His name assures us that He made us capable of knowing enough to experience His salvation. ❧

With God all things are possible.

—Matthew 19:26 NIV

❧

God's love to sinners involves His identifying Himself with their welfare. Such an identification is involved in all love: it is, indeed, the test of whether love is genuine or not.

—J. I. Packer

Words for the Soul

The Word of God is in the Bible as the soul is in the body.

—Peter Taylor Forsyth

8

Soul Food

Hannah Whitall Smith

Be careless in your dress if you must, but keep a tidy soul.

— Mark Twain

What is proper food for the soul? What is the daily bread our Lord would have us to eat? He tells us in that wonderful discourse in the sixth chapter of John, when He says, "I am the bread of life." And adds, "[Whoever] eateth me, even he shall live by me" (John 6:48,57 KJV).

Very few persons realize the effect of thought upon the condition of the soul, that it is in fact food, the substance from which it evolves its strength and health and beauty, or upon which it may become weak and unhealthy and deformed. The things we think about are the things we feed upon. If we think low and corrupt thoughts, we bring disease upon our soul, just as readily as we bring diseases upon our bodies by eating corrupt and improper food.

On the other hand, if we think of Christ we feed on Christ. We eat His flesh and blood practically, by filling our souls with believing thoughts of Him. I know that any who try this plan of filling their souls with believing thoughts of Christ will find they do feed upon Him, as the joy and delight of their hearts. He tells us this when He says, "It is the spirit that quickeneth; the flesh profiteth nothing: the words that I speak unto you, they are spirit, and they are life" (John 6:63 KJV).

It was not His literal flesh they were to eat, but the words that He spake unto them; that is, the truth that He taught them. "Thy words were found, and I did eat them; and thy word was unto me the joy and rejoicing of mine heart: for I am called by thy name, O LORD God of hosts" (Jeremiah 15:16 KJV).

When we take the words of God, that is, His revealed truth, into our lips and eat it; if we dwell upon His words and say them over and over to ourselves, and thoroughly take in and assimilate their meaning in a commonsense way, we find that our soul-life is nourished by them, and is made strong and courageous in consequence. "Finally, brethren, whatsoever things are true, whatsoever things are best, whatsoever things are just, whatsoever things are pure, whatsoever things are lovely, whatsoever things are of good report; if there be any virtue, and if there be any praise, think on these things" (Philippians 4:8).

The things we think on are the things that feed our souls. And the "fruit of our thoughts" are sure to come upon us as the fruit of our actions. ❧

How sweet are your words to my taste,
sweeter than honey to my mouth!

—Psalm 119:103 NIV

❧

God, I praise You for the Bible . . . that Your thoughts are
now available at all times to refresh and nourish and teach me.

—Ruth Myers

9

Fresh Bread Daily

Edith Schaeffer

Break Thou the bread of life, dear Lord, to me,
as Thou didst break the loaves beside the sea.

—Mary A. Lathbury

People were meant to know that, although physical bread had been given by God to satisfy their physical hunger, God's Word was the more important bread. The day-by-day experience of seeing the difference between hunger and satisfaction, the contrast between starved and well-nourished people, is to be immediately transferred by a child of the Living God into recognizing that there is a spiritual parallel which is vital to eternal life. The life-giving words which Jesus was speaking at the time, recorded in John, fit into all that had been taught before.

Here the Messiah, the Second Person of the Trinity, was making it known that He had come to fulfill all the promises and to be the Bread of Life Himself. What He was saying was part of the whole Word of God which was to continue to be daily bread for the spiritually hungry. When we come to the Bread of Life, Jesus Himself, we continue to be fed by "every word that proceedeth out of the mouth of the LORD" (Deuteronomy 8:3 KJV) in His written Word. It is available to be supernaturally kneaded. The ingredients needed for continued strength and help have been mixed in. It has been prepared. Long ago? Yes, but fresh every day.

Come to Isaiah 55:2-3: "Wherefore do ye spend money for that which is not bread? and your labor for that which satisfieth not? hearken diligently unto me, and eat ye that which is good, and let your soul delight itself in fatness. Incline your ear, and come unto me: hear, and your soul shall live" (KJV).

What a beautiful way of giving us a sudden jolt! Are we in danger of spending time and money for something which is not only *not* the Bread of Life, but is helping to destroy the Word of God in some way, by changing what He has blended into it in His perfect wisdom, knowledge, understanding, and love? He has prepared it for His family and the guests who are invited to "taste and see." Have we labored all our hours of one week, one month, or one year to buy material or intellectual things which will diminish our supply of the true bread and the possibility of sharing it with anyone else?

The warning is there, but also the urgent invitation: "Eat ye that which is good." The result of this kind of eating is a delight—and, wonder of wonders, it is to be had without money and without price. Why? Because the price has already been paid for this fantastic supply of fresh bread daily, as well as for the offer to come to Him Who is the Bread of Life. ❧

Then Jesus declared, "I am the bread of life.
He who comes to me will never go hungry,
and he who believes in me will never be thirsty."

—John 6:35 NIV

❧

I am the living bread that came down from heaven.

—Jesus Christ

10

The Bible in Shoe Leather

Oswald Chambers

*The Bible holds up before us ideals that are within sight of
the weakest and the lowliest, and yet so high that the best
and noblest are kept with their faces turned ever upward.*

—William Jennings Bryan

The commandments of our Lord and the conduct of His saints are the counterpart of each other; if they are not, then we are "none of His." The test of truth is the revelation of the Son of God in me, not as a divine anticipation, but as a delightful activity now. It is perilously possible to praise our Lord as Savior and Sanctifier, yet cunningly blind our hearts to the necessity of His manifesting in our mortal flesh His salvation and sanctification.

The Bible tests all experience, all truth, all authority, by our Lord Himself and our relationship to Him personally. It is the confession of conduct. . . . The word "confess" means literally that every bit of my bodily life speaks the same truth as our Lord exhibited in the flesh. It is this scriptural scrutiny that reveals the superb standard of the grace of God. Christian experience is possible only when it is a product of the supernatural grace of God at work in our hearts. . . .

The Holy Spirit alone makes the Word of God understandable. The regenerating and sanctifying work of the Holy Spirit is to incorporate us into Christ until we are living witnesses unto Him. [The preacher] S. D. Gordon put it well when he said, "We have the Bible bound in morocco, bound in all kinds of beautiful leather; what we need is the Bible bound in shoe leather."

That is exactly the teaching of our Lord. After the disciples had received the Holy Spirit they became witnesses to Jesus; their lives spoke more eloquently than their lips—"and they took knowledge of them, that they had been with Jesus" (Acts 4:13 KJV).

The Holy Spirit being imparted to us and expressed through us is the manifested exhibition that God can do all that His Word states He can. It is those who have received that Holy Spirit who understand the will of God and "grow up into him in all things . . ." (Ephesians 4:15 KJV). &

The grass withers and the flowers fall, but the word of our God stands forever.

—Isaiah 40:8 NIV

&

Men do not reject the Bible because it contradicts itself but because it contradicts them.

— The Defender

11

Trembling at His Word

Jean Fleming

Hear the word of the Lord, you who tremble at His word.

— Isaiah the Prophet

&

God wants us to come to the Bible as those who tremble at His words. That means we need to take God seriously and believe God is Who He says He is, that He thinks and acts just as He says. Trembling at His Word is the equivalent to the "fear God" used so often throughout the Scriptures.

Josiah was the kind of "trembler" God esteems. During his reign the long-neglected Book of the Law was found in the Temple. When Josiah heard the message of the book and realized the extent of the nation's disobedience and the judgment that would surely fall on them, he tore his clothes and wept in anguish (2 Kings 22:11).

Josiah came to the scrolls with a prior commitment to obey them with all his heart and soul. He reinstituted celebration of the Passover and began a vigorous campaign to rid the land of false gods. His responsiveness characterizes the man or woman who takes God's Word seriously.

A trembling heart prepares our spirits for greater intimacy with God's Word. As a teenager, E. Stanley Jones, a Methodist missionary to India for fifty years, would press his lips to passages that spoke to his heart. Jones' holy kiss seems to me to express the same spirit the writer of Psalm 119 recorded (NIV): "I rejoice in following your statutes as one rejoices in great riches" (verse 14); "Your statutes are my delight" (verse 24); "How sweet are your words to my taste" (verse 103); "My heart trembles at your word" (verse 161).

When we take God's Word seriously, our hands hover over our Bibles in anticipation. God said His Word is the necessary bread that will satisfy (Isaiah 55:3; Matthew 4:4). It is like snow and rain that comes from heavenly realms to the earth for a purpose. God's Word comes to nourish and refresh, to make fruitful and effective. The Bible is not ineffectual; we can expect something to happen when we receive God's message to us (Isaiah 55:10-11).

A spirit of anticipation banishes a blasé approach to Scripture. A trembling heart does not tolerate the thought that it is okay for mature believers, past the first flushed excitement of life in Christ, to stifle their yawns.

Before you open your Bible, stop! Reflect. Kneel. Pray. This Book is spirit, and you need the indwelling Spirit working in your spirit to receive spiritual truth. The Author of this book is your Interpreter. Who else knows the deep things of God except the Spirit of God? He comes to read to your spirit the language of your Father. ❧

Rulers persecute me without cause,
but my heart trembles at your word.

— Psalm 119:161 NIV

❧

'Twas God the Word that spake it; He took
the Bread and brake it; And what the Word
did make it; That I believe, and take it.

— S. Clarke

12
There Is a Balm

Kay Arthur

Is there no balm in Gilead? Is there no physician there?

—Jeremiah the Prophet

[In Gilead] a balm was produced which was known not only for its healing properties but also for its cosmetic benefits.

Gilead, however, was not only known for the balm it produced. It was also known as a place where people fled when they were in trouble. Jacob fled there from Laban, his father-in-law. The Israelites fled there when being pursued by the Philistines. And David fled there when being pursued by Absalom. Under Moses, it was declared a city of refuge.

O Beloved, as a child of God, where do you run in the time of trouble? Where is your city of refuge? Where is your Gilead?

Over and over again the psalmist describes the varied states of distress in which God's people found themselves. As you read, the tension builds, relieved only by the words, "Then they cried out to the LORD in their trouble; He saved them out of their distresses" (Psalm 107:13 NASB).

Twice we read this phrase, and then we come to verse 17: "Fools, because of their rebellious way, and because of their iniquities, were afflicted. Their soul abhorred all kinds of food; and they drew near to the gates of death. Then they cried out to the LORD in their trouble; He saved them out of their distresses. He sent His word and healed them, and delivered them from their destructions" (Psalm 107:17-20 NASB).

There it is! The Word of God that can heal the soul. You—anyone—can be delivered from your pit of despair because there is a Balm in Gilead, there is a Great Physician there!

In Jeremiah's day God's people had committed two evils. First, they had forsaken God, the fountain of living waters. Second, they had hewn for themselves cisterns, broken cisterns, which wouldn't hold water. In other words, they had turned from God and His ways to the flesh and its ways. They did not draw from Him that which is essential for life—living water.

A cistern is simply a place to store something, usually water. What you put into a cistern is what you get out of it. In contrast, a wellspring has an unseen source from which you draw. The people of Jeremiah's day had forsaken the fountain of living waters for broken cisterns which couldn't even hold water! We do the same thing when we turn from the Word of God to the counsel and wisdom of man for healing our hurts.

You can be healed if you will be healed His way. You can be healed if you will run to Calvary, your city of refuge. Remember, there is a Balm in Gilead and there is a Physician there. ❧

Heal me, O LORD, and I will be healed; save me and I will be saved, for you are the one I praise.

—Jeremiah 17:14 NIV

❧

There is healing through the blood of Christ and deliverance for every captive.

—Smith Wigglesworth

13

The Sword of the Word

Charles Haddon Spurgeon

I follow [the Bible] in all things, both great and small.

—John Wesley

Whenever we feel ourselves dead, and especially in prayer, get close to the Word, for the Word of God is alive. When you have nothing to say to your God, let Him say something to you. The best private devotion is made up, half of searching Scripture in which God speaks to us, and the other half of prayer and praise, in which we speak to God. When you are dead, turn from death to the Word which still lives.

Whenever we feel weak in our duties, let us go to the Word of God and the Christ in the Word for power, and this will be the best of power. The power of our natural abilities, the power of acquired knowledge, the power of our gathered experience, all these may be vanity, but the power which is in the Word will prove effectual. Get up from the cistern of your failing strength to the fountain of omnipotence; for they that drink here, while the youths shall faint and be weary, and the young men shall utterly fall, shall run, and not be weary, and shall walk and not faint.

If you need anything that will cut your hearer to the heart, go to this Book for it. When our hearts grow hot and our words are apt to be sharp as a razor, let us remember that the wrath of man works not the righteousness of God. Let us not attempt to carry on Christ's war with the weapons of Satan.

There is nothing so cutting as the Word of God. Keep to that. I believe also that one of the best ways of convincing men of error is not so much to denounce the error as to proclaim the truth more clearly. If a stick is very crooked, and you wish to prove that it is so, get a straight one, and quietly lay it down by its side, and when men look they will surely see the difference. The Word of God has a very keen edge about it.

When we cannot get at people by God's truth, we cannot get at them at all. I have heard of preachers who have thought they ought to adapt themselves a little to certain people, and leave out portions of the truth which might be disagreeable. If the Word of God will not pierce, our words will not, and you may depend upon that.

Since this Book is meant to be a discerner or critic of the thoughts and intents of the heart, let the Book criticize us. If the Word of God approves you, you are approved; if the Word of God disapproves you, you are disapproved. Have friends praised you? They may be wrong or right, let the Book decide.

Cling you to the living Word, and let the gospel of your fathers, let the gospel of the martyrs, let the gospel of the Reformers, let the gospel of the blood-washed multitude before the throne of God, the gospel of our Lord Jesus Christ, be your gospel. &

For the word of God is living and active. Sharper
than any double-edged sword, it penetrates even
to dividing soul and spirit, joints and marrow;
it judges the thoughts and attitudes of the heart.

—Hebrews 4:12 NIV

&

The Bible is God's chart for you to steer by, to keep you from
the bottom of the sea, and to show you where the harbor is,
and how to reach it without running on rocks and bars.

—Henry Ward Beecher

14

Delighting in the Law

Calvin Miller

Holy Bible, book divine, precious treasure, thou art mine.

—John Burton

As disciples we are to be learners in a continuing affair with the Scripture. No one can be called mature who does not continue to learn; neither can disciples be disciples unless they are gathering day by day an increasing use and understanding of the Word of God.

Again and again the Scriptures teach the importance of study for consistent Christian living. Therefore, happy Christians have no alternative but to learn the Bible. Remember Romans 15:4 (RSV): "For whatever was written in former days was written for our instruction." Remember also God's caution to Israel in Hosea 4:6 (RSV): "My people are destroyed for lack of knowledge." The maturity from which happiness ensues is never easily attained. But we will, with each new plateau of understanding, experience a growing appreciation of how God's Word is the matrix from which the most practical kinds of problems find their solutions.

Paul uses an interesting word in connection with study. It is translated "sound" but it actually means "healthy." First of all, Paul exhorts us to have a healthy reason: "Follow the pattern of the *[healthy]* words which you have heard from me" (2 Timothy 1:13 RSV). Then after beginning with healthy reason, we are to seek out healthy teaching: "He must hold firm to the sure word as taught, so that he may be able to give instruction in healthy doctrine and also to refuse those who contradict it" (Titus 1:9).

The implications of this are tremendous. You can be a healthy Christian only if you are seeking healthy reasons and healthy teaching. It is difficult to find anyone who is both happy and sick. Confident believers must be students, and out of their studies will issue people who are "healthy in faith" (Titus 1:13).

Study, while demanding, is never grievous. The outcome of learning the Bible is a love for its content and a respect for its relevancy. The Word which comes to dwell in our lives is itself the parent of joy. Remember the great first Psalm? It blessed the man whose delight was in the Law of the Lord, especially if the man meditated upon the Word of the Lord. And notice that happiness and security immediately arise from an inward affair with God's Law.

There is a great principle in constant meditation on Scripture. The mind is a narrow channel, capable of focusing on only one thought at a time. Therefore, if the mind is focusing on the Word of God, it cannot focus on any negative or bothersome issue. This in itself is a sound principle of mental or spiritual health. This health develops as we agree to the discipline of our discipleship. &

I meditate on your precepts and consider your ways.
I delight in your decrees; I will not neglect your word.

—Psalm 119:15-16 NIV

&

How glad the heathens would have been, that worship idols,
wood and stone, if they the Book of God had seen.

—Isaac Watts

Pathways to Prayer

In the morning, prayer is the key that opens to us
the treasure of God's mercies and blessings;
in the evening, it is the key that shuts us up
under His protection and safeguard.

—Anonymous

15

Grabbing Aholt of God

Brennan Manning

Prayer is not conquering God's reluctance,
but taking hold of God's willingness.

— Phillips Brooks

❦

"I don't see why anyone should settle for anything less than Jacob," writes Walker Percy, "who actually *grabbed aholt* of God and wouldn't let go until God identified Himself and blessed him."

Many Christians never have grabbed aholt of God. They do not know, really know, that God dearly and passionately loves them. Many accept it theoretically, others in a shadowy sort of way. While their belief system is invulnerable, their faith in God's love for them is remote and abstract.

How do we grab aholt of God? How do we overcome our sadness and isolation? How do we develop the courage and generosity to treasure the signature of Jesus on the pages of our lives? How, how, how! The answer comes irresistibly and unmistakably: prayer.

Whatever else it may be, prayer is first and foremost an act of love. Beyond any pragmatic considerations, prayer is a personal response to the love of God. To love someone implies a longing for presence and communion. "Yet the news about him spread all the more, so that crowds of people came to hear him and to be healed of their sicknesses. But Jesus often withdrew to lonely places and prayed" (Luke

5:15-16 NIV). Jesus prayed primarily because He loved His Father. To be like Christ is to be a Christian.

No matter how overextended we are, we manage to make time for the people who matter to us. The readiness to conscientiously waste time with a friend is a silent affirmation of their importance in our lives.

Basil Pennington, in his book *Centering Prayer,* captures the simplicity of this gesture: "A father is delighted when his little one, leaving off his toys and friends, runs to him and climbs into his arms. As he holds his little one close to him, he cares little whether the child is looking around, his attention flitting from one thing to another, or just settling down to sleep. Essentially the child is choosing to be with his father, confident of the love, the care, the security, that is there in those arms.

"Contemplative prayer is something like that. We settle down in our Father's arms, in His loving hands. Our mind, our thoughts, our imagination may flit about here and there; we might even fall asleep; but essentially we are choosing to remain for this time intimately with our Father, giving ourselves to Him, receiving His love and care, letting Him enjoy us as He will."

One of the four cardinal rules in prayer is: Pray as you can; don't pray as you can't. We must find our own way. ✤

If you, then, though you are evil, know how to give good gifts to your children, how much more will your Father in heaven give good gifts to those who ask him!

—Matthew 7:11 NIV

✤

What matters is the faith which lays hold on God.

—Dietrich Bonhoeffer

16

Enjoying God in Prayer

Jeanne Guyon

*When thou prayest, rather let thy heart be
without words than thy words without heart.*

—John Bunyan

Let all pray. You should live by prayer as you should live by love. This is very easily obtained, much more easily than you can conceive. Come, you famishing souls who find nothing to satisfy you. Come, and you shall be filled. Come, you poor, afflicted ones, bending beneath your load of wretchedness and pain, and you shall be comforted! Come, you sick, to your physician, and don't be fearful of approaching Him because you are filled with diseases. Show them, and they shall be healed!

Children, draw near to your Father and He will embrace you in the arms of love. Come, you poor, stray, wandering sheep, return to your Shepherd! Come, sinners, to your Savior! Come, you who are dull, ignorant and illiterate, and who think yourselves most incapable of prayer. You are most especially adapted for it. Let all without exception come, for Jesus Christ has called all.

Yet let not those come who are without a heart, for they are excused. There must be a heart before there can be love. But who is without a heart? Oh, come then, give this heart to God and learn here how to make that donation.

All who desire prayer may do so easily, enabled by those ordinary graces and gifts of the Holy Spirit which are common to all men. Prayer is the sovereign good. It is the means of delivering us from every vice, and obtaining every virtue. It is by prayer alone that we are brought in God's presence and maintained in it without interruption.

You must learn, then, a kind of prayer that may be exercised at all times, a kind that does not obstruct outward employments, and may be practiced equally by princes, kings, prelates, priests and magistrates, soldiers and children, tradesmen, laborers, women, and sick persons. It is the prayer not of the head but of the heart. Nothing can interrupt this prayer but disordered affections; and when once we have enjoyed God and the sweetness of His love, we shall find it impossible to relish anything but Himself.

Nothing is so easily obtained as the possession and enjoyment of God. He is more present to us than we are to ourselves. He is more desirous of giving Himself to us than we are to possess Him. We need only to know how to seek Him, and the way is easier and more natural to us than breathing.

Listen! You who think yourselves to be so dull and fit for nothing! By prayer you may live on God Himself with less difficulty or interruption than you live in the vital air. Wouldn't it seem, then, to be highly sinful to neglect prayer? ஒ

Be joyful always; pray continually.
—1 Thessalonians 5:16-17 NIV

ஒ

Prayer is exhaling the spirit of man
and inhaling the Spirit of God.
—Edwin Keith

17

Praying the Ordinary

Richard J. Foster

*Pray to God at the beginning of all thy works that
thou mayest bring them all to a good ending.*

—Xenophon

Anthony Bloom wrote, "A prayer makes sense only if it is lived. Unless they are lived, unless life and prayer become completely interwoven, prayers become a sort of polite madrigal which you offer to God at moments when you are giving time to Him."

The work of our hands and of our minds is acted-out prayer, a love offering to the living God. In what is perhaps the finest line in the movie *Chariots of Fire,* Olympic runner Eric Liddell tells his sister, "Jenny, when I run I feel His pleasure." This is the reality that is to permeate all vocations whether we are writing a novel or cleaning a latrine.

It is at latrine cleaning that many have a problem. It is not hard to see how a Michelangelo or a T. S. Eliot is giving glory to God—theirs are creative vocations. But what about the boring jobs, the unimportant jobs, the mundane jobs? How are those prayer?

Here we must understand the order in the kingdom of God. It is precisely in the slop-bucket job—the work that we abhor—where we will find God the most. We do not need to have good feelings or a warm glow to do work for the glory of God. All good work is pleasing to the Father. Even the jobs that seem meaningless and mindless to us are highly valued in the order of the kingdom of God.

God values the ordinary. If, for the glory of God, you are putting an endless supply of nuts on an endless line of bolts, your work is rising up as sweet-smelling sacrifices to the throne of God. He is pleased with your labor.

We also "pray the ordinary" when we engage in what Jean-Nicholas Grou calls the prayer of action. He says, "Every action performed in the sight of God because it is the will of God, and in the manner that God wills, is a prayer and indeed a better prayer than could be made in words at such times."

Each activity of daily life in which we stretch ourselves on behalf of others is a prayer of action—the times when we scrimp and save to get the children something special; the times when we share our car with others on rainy mornings, leaving early to get them to work on time; the times when we keep up correspondence with friends or answer one last telephone call when we are dead tired at night. These times and many more like them are lived prayer. Ignatius of Loyola notes, "Everything that one turns in the direction of God is prayer." &o

Men ought always to pray, and not to faint.

—Luke 18:1 KJV

&o

Prayer is not merely an occasional impulse to which we respond when we are in trouble: prayer is a life attitude.

—Walter A. Mueller

18

Abiding Prayer

Andrew Murray

The deepest wishes of the heart find expression in secret prayer.
— George E. Rees

Prayer is both one of the means and one of the fruits of union with Christ. As a means it is of unspeakable importance. All the things of faith, all the pleading of desire, all the yearning after a full surrender, all the confessions of shortcomings and sin, all the exercises in which the soul gives up itself and clings to Christ, find their utterance in prayer. It is the believer who takes time in secret prayer and waits until he has laid hold of what he has seen, who grows strong in Christ.

Christ does not think of prayer as a means of getting blessings for ourselves, but as one of the chief channels of influence by which the blessings of Christ's redemption are dispensed to the world. He assures us that if we abide in Him, we shall have power with God and man. Ours shall be the effectual, fervent prayer of the righteous man, availing much. Such prayer will be the fruit of our abiding in Him, and the means of bringing forth much fruit.

Abiding in Christ, I can fully avail myself of the nature of Christ. Asking in the name of another means he has authorized me to ask, and wants to be considered as asking himself. The promise, "Whatsoever ye ask in my name. . ." (John 14:13) may not be severed from the command,

"Whatsoever ye do . . . do all in the name of the Lord Jesus" (Colossians 3:17 KJV).

If the name of Christ is to be wholly at my disposal, it must be because I first put myself wholly at His disposal so He has free and full command of me.

It is the abiding in Christ that gives the right and power to use His name with confidence. To Christ, the Father refuses nothing. Abiding in Christ, I come to the Father as one with Him. His righteousness is in me, His Spirit in me. The Father sees the Son in me and gives me my petition. Abiding in Christ not only renews my will to pray aright, but secures the full power of His merits to me.

Believer, abide in Christ, for there is the school of prayer— mighty, effectual, answer-bringing prayer. Abide in Him, and you shall learn that the secret of the prayer of faith is the life of faith—the life that abides in Christ alone. ❧

But when you pray, go into your room, close the door and pray to your Father, who is unseen. Then your Father, who sees what is done in secret, will reward you.

—Matthew 6:6 NIV

❧

Prayer is not only "the practice of the presence of God," it is the realization of His presence.

—Joseph Fort Newton

19
Waiting on God

Gordon Macdonald

*Prayer is a rising up and a drawing near to God in mind,
and in heart, and in spirit.*

—Alexander Whyte

We need a period of preparatory time before our souls are ready to engage in heavenly intimacy. I imagine the soul as something that hides from all the noise and busyness of life. Can I suggest that it has to be coaxed into action? And the coaxing may take time that most of us do not think we have.

We all have been taught the importance of daily prayer. But I suspect we could profit more from a weekly experience of three or four prayerful hours than just a few minutes each day. It's not a fair comparison, perhaps, but my intuition suggests that I'm "righter-than-wronger" about this.

When I was younger, my impatience was troublesome. I would privately observe to my wife that I saw little connection between my prayers and the results. This was the conclusion of a small thinker with too few years of life under his belt, one who could not see things over the long haul.

Today is different. Fifty-plus years is not exactly a long view, but it is long enough to realize that what one says from the soul must be cast in the perspective of eternity, and the promises and purposes of God. I am praying prayers that may not have their answer until long after I'm in the grave. And that's okay. I know now that God never has been oblivious of one word I've spoken from the soul in His direction. The timing is His; the patience must be mine.

The Mysterious One to Whom we direct our souls moves with agonizing slowness on some days and with lightning speed on others. In prayer we lay no demands, no time-lines, and no measurements before Him. We bow, speak the language of the soul, and then wait, often without telling others what we wait for. Conversation from soul to heaven is enough.

I am bothered by the thought that silence, time touched with the spiritual ancients, self-disclosure in a journal, and patience are not commodities in great supply today. In part, that is why our prayers may take the form of shallow words, empty clichés, quick-burst comments, and religious soliloquies.

Give me the soul talk of prayer any time! Ten words of it are worth a thousand of the other kind. Soul talk is that which comes from the bottom of our inner world. It is where God is likely to dwell through union with Christ, and we reach for His grace. It is where we look at creation and its possibilities with fresh eyes and worship. It is where we come to understand that every minute spent in the Divine Presence is worth infinitely more than gold. ❧

Wait for the LORD; be strong and
take heart and wait for the LORD.

— Psalm 27:14 NIV

❧

The most important thing in any prayer is not what we say to God, but what God
says to us. We are apt to pray and then
hurry away without giving God a chance to answer.

— Christian Advocate

20
A Dangerous Business

Peter Marshall

Praying is dangerous business. Results do come.

— G. Christi Swain

The prayer of faith can move mountains. It can heal the sick. It can overcome the world. It can work miracles. It "availeth much."

It is like the atomic bomb in at least two particulars. It may be just as dangerous. And it certainly is as little explored.

Believers have not experimented with prayer, regarding it as an emergency measure or a conventional practice to be maintained, much as one's subscription to a series of culture lectures. It is culture—and not conviction—that keeps some people praying.

The whole field of prayer, and praying as laying hold of unlimited power, is unexplored, with the result that spiritual laws still lie undiscovered by the average believer.

There is an element of danger and risk in all exploration into new fields. Every scientist knows that. Every explorer into the realm of the spiritual will find it just as true.

[One spiritual law] is that we must seek and be willing to accept the will of God—whatever it may be for us. Our prayers must not be efforts to bend God to our will or desires—but yield ourselves to His—whatever they may be.

We forget that God sometimes has to say, "No." We pray to Him as our Heavenly Father, and like wise human fathers, He often says, "No," not from whim or caprice, but from wisdom and from love, and knowing what is best for us.

Christ Himself, in the agony of the Garden of Gethsemane, prayed with the certain stipulation that God's will—not His—be done. It is this factor of divine decision which the skeptic cannot comprehend, and which the believer must accept, that produces answered prayer.

It is this matter of the surrender of our wills to God's will that is hard for us. It is this unknown factor—sometimes not knowing what is God's will in a particular case—that makes praying dangerous business. Usually we learn how wonderful God's will really is only through experience.

Just as soon as we are willing to accept God's decision in the matter about which we are praying, whatever it may turn out to be, then, and not until then, will our prayers be answered. For God is always far more willing to give us good things than we are anxious to receive them.

It is also dangerous business to pray for something unless you really and truly mean it. You see, God might call your bluff, take you up on it . . . and would you be surprised! ❧

Lord, teach us to pray.

—Luke 11:1 NIV

❧

Spread out your petition before God, and then say,
"Thy will be done." The sweetest lesson I have learned
in God's school is to let the Lord choose for me.

—Dwight L. Moody

21
Fuel for the Flame

John White

Whatever a man prays for, he prays for a miracle.

—Van Sergeyevich Turgenev

❦

Prayer is a fire which needs fuel to burn and a match to light it. If the fire burns low we can fan it so the flame may burn more fiercely. But all the fanning in the world cannot create a bonfire from a single match nor from a pile of dead, cold fuel.

Fire must come from above; indeed He has already come. The Holy Spirit burns quietly within the Christian ready to light the fuel of Scripture's truth. But the fuel must be there.

If we would intercede for others, then we must soak our minds in Scripture that the Holy Spirit may have fuel to light within us. There must be plenty of fuel, not just isolated texts chosen at random. The fuel has to be thick and heavy. Promises may catch alight quickly, but for a lasting fire we will need some solid knowledge about the nature and the character of God and of His Christ and their intervention in human history. Straw may produce a brilliant flash, but we will need logs for sustained burning.

Let me put the matter another way. We cannot pray fervently without faith and hope. If we approach a door expecting that no one will be at home or fearing that whoever is at home will receive us coldly, we may not be inclined to knock more than once. On the other hand the fact that we may have been received with frequent kindness will give us the faith and hope to knock hard a second time.

And in the same way, faith and hope in God bring prayer alive and make it persistent. Both virtues, faith and hope, come to us in the measure that Scripture is stored in our minds and hearts. If then we want to know what it means to have prayers that burn with hope, or if, putting it another way, we want to knock on the door expectantly, we will need a mind molded by Scripture.

I must not leave the impression that we should only pray when we burn in blessed ecstasy. We may need to fan the flames of prayer, even to fan them long and hard. We are not excused from duty because our feelings do not accommodate themselves to it.

Fanning the flames, then, means meditating upon Scripture, affirming our confidence before God in its reliability, praising Him for its content and asking Him whether the truths we meditate on do not indeed apply to those for whom we pray.

It may please the Holy Spirit on occasion to cause a sudden uprush of flame from the material, so that fanning becomes unnecessary. The fuel in other words may or may not need to be fanned, but the fuel must be present if it is to burn. &

Ask whatever you wish, and it will be given you.

—John 15:7

&

A man is continually at prayer when he lives according to truth.

—Emanuel Swedenborg

Everyday Faith

Faith is to believe, on the Word of God,
what we do not see, and its reward is
to see and enjoy what we believe.

—St. Augustine

22

Dare to Trust God

Catherine Marshall

*Trusting in Him who can go with me and
remain in you, and be everywhere for good,
let us confidently hope that all will yet be well.*

—Abraham Lincoln

"Now don't push the term *faith* at me," a lawyer told me bluntly at a dinner party recently. "The word is like a red flag."

"Why such a violent reaction?" I asked.

"Well, because I object to the way people use faith as a theological gimmick to duck all rational problems. At every point where a man wants to understand, they say, 'You just have to have faith,' or, 'Reason only goes so far.' I resent it! I see nothing wrong with 'Prove it to me first, then I'll believe.'"

As we talked, I realized that it had never occurred to this intelligent, well-educated man that in his everyday life he often follows the reverse order—belief and acceptance first, then action. Every day he lives, he acts on faith many times with little proof or none at all, and he does not feel that he is being impractical.

He demonstrates an act of faith each time he boards a plane. He believes that it will take him to his destination, but he has no proof of it. He entrusts life itself to several unknown mechanics who have serviced the plane, as well as to a pilot about whom he knows nothing.

Each time he eats a meal in a restaurant he trusts some unknown cook behind the scenes and eats the food on faith,

faith that it is not contaminated. He enters a hospital for an operation and signs a release giving permission for surgery. This is an act of faith in an anesthetist whose name he may not even know and a surgeon who holds in his hands the power of life or death.

He accepts a prescription from a doctor and takes it to a druggist, thus activating his faith that the pharmacist will fill the prescription accurately. The use of the wrong drug might be deadly, but he is not equipped to analyze the contents before swallowing the pill.

It is obvious that if we insisted on the "proof first, then faith" order in our daily lives, organized life as we know it would grind to a screeching halt. And since life together among people is possible only by faith, as we act out trust in others, it should not seem odd that the same law applies to our life with God.

In the spiritual realm, when for some reason or other we refuse to act by faith, all activity stops just as completely as it does in the secular realm. There is no way for us even to take the first steps toward the spiritual life except by faith, any more than a baby can get launched on his earthly life without blind baby-trust in his parents and other adults. We accept the fact of a personal relationship with God by faith, even as our young children accept the fact of parental love. ☙

Now faith is being sure of what we hope for
and certain of what we do not see.

—Hebrews 11:1 NIV

☙

How calmly may we commit ourselves to the hands of
Him Who bears up the world.

—Jean Paul Richter

23

Trusting in a Person

Michael Griffiths

It is never a question with any of us of faith or not faith;
the question always is, "In what or in whom do we put our faith?"

—Anonymous

&

There can be few people who do not know that being a Christian has something to do with faith. However, not many people could define clearly what they mean by faith, and still fewer could explain exactly what Christians mean by it.

Emerson said faith is the rejection of a lesser fact and the acceptance of a greater. Christians say that God is that greater fact.

It has been said that faith is our response to God's initiative. It means responding to God even when it is difficult to do so.

Jesus told a story that illustrates this beautifully: "Two men went up to the temple to pray, one a Pharisee and the other a tax collector. The Pharisee stood up and prayed about himself: 'God, I thank you that I am not like other men—robbers, evildoers, adulterers—or even like this tax collector. I fast twice a week and give a tenth of all I get.'

"But the tax collector stood at a distance. He would not even look up to heaven, but beat his breast and said, 'God, have mercy on me, a sinner.' I tell you that this man, rather than the other, went home justified before God. For everyone who exalts himself will be humbled, and he who humbles himself will be exalted" (Luke 18:10-14 NIV).

The Bible says that the tax collector went home justified before God. So does God justify a bad man, but reject a good man? The key is to ask very simply, "Who is trusting whom?" The Pharisee's religion is reminiscent of what we sometimes rather rudely call "public school religion." If you lead a decent life and are a decent, nice person, then God, Who is also a nice, decent Person, will accept you. That Pharisee was trusting in his own good character. Clearly, he was not really trusting in God, even though he prayed to Him. Instead, he was trusting in himself.

Listen now to the other man: "God, have mercy on me, a sinner." Who is this man trusting in? He cannot trust in his own character—he knows he is a sinner. He cannot trust in his own worthy actions—he has sinned. He puts all his confidence, therefore, in the character and actions of God. God is a God Whose character is merciful, Who has mercy upon sinners.

Do you begin to see what Christians mean by *faith?* They mean trust in Somebody else: depending on God. A Christian is somebody who trusts in the holiness and righteousness of God and, particularly, in what God has done in Christ, reconciling the world to Himself by Jesus' death on the cross. A Christian's trust is not in his own character or actions but in the character and actions of God. &

Have faith in God.

—Mark 11:22 KJV

&

Faith is a knowledge of the benevolence of God toward us, and a certain persuasion of His veracity.

—John Calvin

24
The Lovely Will of God

Hannah Whitall Smith

Faith is saying "Amen" to God.

—Merv Rosell

I have learned to know beyond the shadow of doubt, that the will of God is the most delicious and delightful thing in the universe. And this, not because things always go as I want them to go, neither because of any extra piety on my part, but simply because my common sense tells me that the will of unselfish love could not be anything else but delightful. The reason heaven is heaven is because God's will is perfectly done there.

I had been used to hearing Christians talk about consecration to the will of God as being such a high religious attainment that only a few extra devout souls could hope to reach it. But with my discovery of the infinite unselfishness of God, I came to realize that consecration to Him was not an attainment but a priceless privilege; and I cannot but feel sure that if people only knew the loveliness of His will, not a devout few only, but every soul in the universe would rush eagerly to choose it for every moment of their lives.

This seems to me to be not an extra degree of piety, but only an extra degree of good sense. If I were lost in a trackless wilderness and could see no way out, and a skillful guide should offer to lead me into safety, would I consider it a hard thing to surrender myself into his hands, and say, "Thy will be done" to his guidance? And can it be a hard thing to surrender myself to my Heavenly Guide, and say, "Thy will be done" to His guidance?

No, a thousand times no! Consecration, or as I prefer to call it, surrender to God, is the greatest privilege offered to any soul in this life, and to say, "Thy will be done" is one of the most delightful things human lips are allowed to utter.

An old writer has said that God's will is not a load to carry, as so many think, but is a pillow to rest on, and I found this to be true. My soul sank back upon it with a sweetness of contented rest that no words can describe. At other times, to say the words "Thy will be done" seemed to me like a magnificent shout of victory, a sort of triumphant banner, flung forth in the face of the whole universe, challenging it to combat.

But time would fail me to tell of all that my soul discovered when I discovered the goodness and unselfishness of God. To say that He is enough is to give an absolute and incontrovertible answer to every doubt and every question that has arisen or can arise. I had begun to discover that He actually was all I needed; and that even infinitely more than all, beyond what I could ask or think, was stored up for me in Him. ❧

Our Father in heaven, hallowed be your name, your kingdom come, your will be done on earth as it is in heaven.

—Matthew 6:9-10 NIV

❧

And in His will is our peace.

—Dante Alighieri

25

Freedom to Trust

Eugene Peterson

Don't try to hold God's hand; let Him hold yours.
Let Him do the holding, and you the trusting.

—Hammer William Webb-Peploe

The famous promise to Abraham was that he would be the father of the faithful and that all the nations of the earth would be blessed in his offspring. But there was a problem: Abraham did not have a child. All he had was a promise that he would have a child.

The years piled up. Still no child. God promised but there was nothing to show for it. Besides, there was a biological absurdity at the heart of the whole business: Sarah was an old woman, and barren.

If ever there was a situation in which it seemed like a clear case for God helping those who help themselves, this was it. Abraham and Sarah, unable to conceive a child, conceived a plan: Sarah's young maid, Hagar, would bear the child. The plan was full of common sense. It was agreed and acted upon. Hagar became pregnant and Ishmael was born.

A few years later Sarah conceived and gave birth to Isaac.

One son was born because God promised, the other son was born because Abraham and Sarah doubted. The great disaster of Abraham's life was that he used Hagar to get what he thought God wanted for him; the great achievement of his life was what God did for him apart from any programs or plans that he put into action.

The lesson of that old piece of history is clear enough: the moment we begin manipulating lives in order to get control of circumstances, we become enslaved in our own plans, tangled up in our own red tape, and have to live with grievous, unintended consequences. The life of freedom is a life of receiving, of believing, of accepting, of hoping. Because God freely keeps His promises, we are free to trust.

No one has understood this better than Paul. He knew that we are not whole persons until we are free, and that we are not free until we trust. He faced the reality that religion repeatedly falls prey to the insatiable will of human beings to do and control and thus makes a mockery of that freedom. And he proclaimed, with rare power and effectiveness, that God in Christ has set us free from that compulsion that we can be free in the original created sense: free to live in a praising, trusting relationship with God, free to live in a loving, serving relationship with other persons. &

In God I trust; I will not be afraid. What can man do to me?

—Psalm 56:11 NIV

&

*You may trust the Lord too little
but you can never trust Him too much.*

—Anonymous

26

Leave It to God

C. S. Lewis

All I have seen teaches me to trust the Creator for all I have not seen.

—Ralph Waldo Emerson

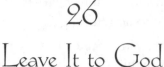

When the most important things in our life happen we quite often do not know, at the moment, what is going on. A man does not always say to himself, "Hello! I'm growing up!" You can see it even in simple matters. A man who starts anxiously watching to see whether he is going to sleep is very likely to remain wide awake.

As well, the [change] I am talking of now may not happen to every one in a sudden flash—like St. Paul or Bunyan: it may be so gradual that no one could ever point to a particular hour or even a particular year. What matters is the nature of the change in itself, not how we feel while it is happening. It is the change from being confident about our own efforts to the state in which we despair of doing anything for ourselves and leave it to God.

I know the words "leave it to God" can be misunderstood. The sense in which a Christian leaves it to God is that he puts all his trust in Christ: trust that Christ will somehow share with him the perfect human obedience which He carried out from His birth to His crucifixion: that Christ will make the man more like Himself and, in a sense, make good his deficiencies. In Christian language, He will share His sonship with us, will make us, like Himself, sons of God.

If you like to put it that way, Christ offers something for nothing; He even offers everything for nothing. In a sense, the whole Christian life consists in accepting that very remarkable offer. But the difficulty is to reach the point of recognizing that all we have done and can do is nothing.

What we should have liked would be for God to count our good points and ignore our bad ones. Again, in a sense, you may say that no temptation is ever overcome until we stop trying to remove it—throw up the sponge. But then you could not "stop trying" in the right way and for the right reason until you had tried your very hardest.

There would be no sense in saying you trusted a person if you would not take his advice. Thus, if you have really handed yourself over to Him, it must follow that you are trying to obey Him. But trying in a new way, a less worried way. Not doing these things in order to be saved, but because He has begun to save you already. Not hoping to get heaven as a reward for your actions, but inevitably wanting to act in a certain way because a first faint gleam of heaven is already visible to you. &

Trust in him at all times, O people; pour out
your hearts to him, for God is our refuge.

—Psalm 62:8 NIV

We trust as we love, and where we love.
If we love Christ much, surely we shall trust Him much.

—Thomas Benton Brooks

27

Have Faith in God

Smith Wigglesworth

Faith is the daring of the soul to go farther than it can see.

—William Newton Clarke

These are days when we need to have our faith strengthened, when we need to know God. God has designed that the just shall live by faith. Any man can be changed by faith, no matter how he may be fettered. I know that God's Word is sufficient. One word from Him can change a nation. His Word is from everlasting to everlasting.

It is through the entrance of this everlasting Word, this incorruptible seed, that we are born again and come into this wonderful salvation. Man cannot live by bread alone, but must live by every word that proceeds out of the mouth of God. This is the food of faith. Faith comes by hearing, and hearing by the Word of God.

I tell you God can arrange everything without going near. He can plan for you, and when He plans for you, all is peace. All things are possible if you will believe. All the impossibility is with us when we measure God by the limitations of our unbelief.

"What things soever ye desire, when ye pray, believe that ye receive them, and ye shall have them" (Mark 11:24 KJV). Desire toward God, and you will have desires from God; and

He will meet you on the line of those desires when you reach out in simple faith.

Did you believe before you were saved? So many people would be saved, but they want to feel saved first. There was never a man who felt saved before he believed. God's plan is always this: If you will believe, you shall see the glory of God. I believe God wants to bring us all to a definite place of unswerving faith and confidence in Himself.

Jesus uses the figure of a mountain. Why does He say a mountain? Because if faith can remove a mountain, it can remove anything. The plan of God is so marvelous that if you will only believe, all things are possible.

We have a Jesus Who heals the brokenhearted, Who lets the captives go free, Who saves the very worst. Listen again to this Word of Him Who left the glory to bring us this great salvation: "Verily I say unto you, That whosoever shall say unto this mountain, Be thou removed . . . he shall have whatsoever he saith" (Mark 11:23 KJV).

Whatsoever! &

And without faith it is impossible to please God,
because anyone who comes to him must believe that he
exists and that he rewards those who earnestly seek him.

—Hebrews 11:6 NIV

Trust God for great things; with your five loaves and two fishes,
He will show you a way to feed thousands.

—Horace Bushnell

28

Faith's New Perspective

Paul Little

Faith is the force of life.

— Leo Tolstoy

Faith recognizes the fact that God is in control of my life. Whether I believe it or not, it's a fact that God is in control of the world. If I don't believe it, I'm just robbing myself of the enjoyment of the fact. But if I meditate on this fact and lay hold of it, my fears about the future vanish. Our faith enables us to enjoy and rest in the certainty of His providence.

Faith gives our lives amazingly new perspective. Faith acknowledges God's sovereign control but is not fatalistic. Fatalism submits to a blind, impersonal force over which man has no control. Faith in the providence of God yields willingly to a loving Heavenly Father, Who sees the two sparrows that fall to the ground and Who numbers the hairs of each head. Faith is a far cry from fatalism and in that difference there is great comfort.

Faith encounters many challenges. Dr. Edward Carnell likens the Christian to a physicist watching a magic show. Each successful trick threatens the physicist's faith in the law of uniformity. He may admittedly be baffled, but his faith is not overthrown because the law of uniformity depends on scientific rather than private grounds.

Similarly, the Christian's faith is strengthened as he keeps the promises of God before him and considers, not the difficulties in the way of the things promised, but the character and resources of God Who has made the promise. Job did just this in response to his wife's taunts when God seemed to have abandoned him to incredible suffering. "Don't be an idiot. Curse God and die!" But Job declared, "Though He slay me, yet will I trust Him" (Job 13:15 NKJV).

Habakkuk was bewildered by the events of his day. Judah lay in moral ruin, but God wasn't judging the people. When the prophet asked, "How come?" the Lord answered him, "I'm going to use Chaldea to chastise them." Habakkuk found it even harder to swallow that explanation, for Chaldea was more wicked than Judah.

Habakkuk had to learn to take the long view of God in His dealings with men.

Only then could he confidently affirm, "Though there be no external manifestation of Thy presence and power, O God, I will trust in Thee. Though there be no figs on the tree, no cattle in the stalls, yet will I joy in the Lord and praise the God of my salvation" (Habakkuk 3:17-18). We see faith here, not wishful thinking.

Faith recognizes the realities that have now been revealed in the Lord Jesus Christ; faith takes hold of them and lives in their light. ✥

Fight the good fight of the faith. Take hold of the
eternal life to which you were called when you made
your good confession in the presence of many witnesses.

—1 Timothy 6:12 NIV

✥

Faith lights us through the dark to Deity.

—Edward Young

Grace for Today

There is nothing but God's grace.
We walk upon it; we breathe it;
we live and die by it.

—Robert Louis Stevenson

29

The Gospel of the Second Chance

Max Lucado

Pardon, not wrath, is God's best attribute.

— Bayard Taylor

It was like discovering the prize in a box of Cracker Jacks™ or spotting a little pearl in a box of buttons or stumbling across a ten dollar bill in a drawer full of envelopes.

Look in Mark, chapter 16. Read the first five verses about the women's surprise when they find the stone moved to the side. Then feast on that beautiful phrase spoken by the angel, "He is not here, He is risen," but don't pause for too long. Go a bit further. Get your pencil ready and enjoy this jewel in the seventh verse. It reads like this: "But go, tell His disciples and Peter that He is going before you to Galilee."

If I might paraphrase the words, "Don't stay here, go tell the disciples," a pause, then a smile, "and *especially* tell Peter, that He is going before you to Galilee."

What a line. It's as if all of heaven had watched Peter fall— and it's as if all of heaven wanted to help him back up again. "Be sure and tell Peter that he's not left out. Tell him that one failure doesn't make a flop."

Sure you can have a second chance.

Just ask Peter. Even the angels wanted this distraught netcaster to know that it wasn't over. The message came loud and clear from the Celestial Throne Room through the divine courier. "Be sure and tell Peter that he gets to bat again."

Those who know these types of things say that the Gospel of Mark is really the transcribed notes and dictated thoughts of Peter. If this is true, then it was Peter himself who included these two words! And if these really are his words, I can't help but imagine that the old fisherman had to brush away a tear and swallow a lump when he got to this point in the story.

It's not every day that you get a second chance. Peter must have known that. The next time he saw Jesus, he got so excited that he barely got his britches on before he jumped into the cold water of the Sea of Galilee. It was also enough, so they say, to cause this backwoods Galilean to carry the gospel of the second chance all the way to Rome where they killed him. If you've ever wondered what would cause a man to be willing to be crucified upside down, maybe now you know.

It's not every day that you find someone who will give you a second chance—much less someone who will give you a second chance every day.

But in Jesus, Peter found both. &

But God demonstrates his own love for us in this:
While we were still sinners, Christ died for us. Since we
have now been justified by his blood, how much more
shall we be saved from God's wrath through him!

— Romans 5:8-9 NIV

&

God forgives not capriciously, but with wise, definite,
divine pre-arrangement; forgives universally, on the grounds of
an atonement and on the condition of repentance and faith.

— Richard Salter Storrs

30

The Scandal of the Cross

Dan Allender

The cross is the only ladder high enough to touch heaven's threshold.

— George Dana Boardman

The scandal of the cross is that it is so foolish. God, the infinite Creator, becomes a perfect sacrifice for the sake of a twisted human soul. He not only dies, but does so as a public spectacle of shame.

The separation of God from God is heard in the awful cry of dereliction, "My God, My God, why have you forsaken me?" (Matthew 27:46 NIV). At that moment, as the Son became sin, the Father turned His eyes away in the agony of hatred and love, full of sorrow and joy. It was the most inconceivable moment in the history of being. In the moment of tragic defeat, our foolish God revealed the wonder of His wisdom, passion, and might.

The effect was to destroy the power of the Evil One. The cross was not only our open door to life, but it was the final nail that sealed the Evil One's fate. Paul rejoiced: "When you were dead in your sins and in the uncircumcision of your sinful nature, God made you alive with Christ. He forgave us all our sins, having canceled the written code, with its regulations, that was against us and that stood opposed to us; he took it away, nailing it to the cross. And having disarmed the powers and authorities, he made a public spectacle of them, triumphing over them by the cross" (Colossians 2:13-15 NIV).

The victory of the cross is the triumph of God, the grand paradox. In the most humiliating, inconceivable loss imaginable, God, in fact, triumphs over His enemy and shames the Evil One.

Whatever change occurs in us by our absorption of the implications of Christ's death and resurrection the final act of the play is already scripted. We can relax. Although God's holiness and His law are relentlessly demanding and we cannot, at any moment, live righteously enough in our own holiness to please Him, He provides a way of escape through offering His Son as a covering for our sin. Now, when we are caught in sin, He embraces us, the sinners, as His own sons. He sees us wrapped in the righteousness of His Son and loves who we are and who we will become. We can rejoice.

This is the framework for offering forgiveness and reconciliation to others. God in Christ models for us a wild, reckless, passionate pursuit of the offender by the offended for the sake of the most shame-free party known to man. If one has been forgiven much, then one will learn to boldly pursue through every possible means the one who has done him harm.

The path will be unlike any other journey. It is a path marked by quiet repentance, stunned joy, and passionate celebration. It is a path that leads both forgiver and forgiven into the heart of God. ❧

May I never boast except in the cross of our Lord Jesus Christ, through which the world has been crucified to me, and I to the world.

— Galatians 6:14 NIV

In the cross there is safety.

—Thomas á Kempis

31
Living by Grace

Jerry Bridges

As grace is first from God, so it is continually from Him.

—Jonathan Edwards

The New Testament is replete with assurances of God's forgiveness to those who have trusted in Jesus Christ. Just one Scripture will suffice to show again the contrast between our dreadful condition and God's love, mercy, and grace in reaching out to us. It is, incidentally, another instance of God's wonderful "buts."

Colossians 1:21-22 says, "Once you were alienated from God and were enemies in your minds by your evil behavior. But now he has reconciled you by Christ's physical body through death to present you holy in his sight, without blemish and free from accusation."

I want to call your attention to the last phrase of this passage, "free from accusation." Does this phrase describe the way you think about yourself? Or do you often, in your mind, find yourself standing in the dock of God's courtroom hearing His pronouncement, "Guilty"? If the latter is true, you are not living by grace.

If you have trusted Christ as your Savior, then all the expressions of God's forgiveness are true of you. He has removed your sins as far as the east is from the west. He has put them behind His back and hurled them into the depths of the sea. He has blotted them out of His record book and promised never to bring them up again. You are free from accusation, not because of anything whatsoever in you, but because of His grace alone through Jesus Christ.

Are you willing to believe this wonderful truth and live by it? You probably reply, "I do believe it. I do believe my sins are forgiven and I will go to heaven when I die." But are you willing to *live* by it today, in this life? Will you accept that God not only *saves* you by His grace through Christ but also *deals* with you day by day by His grace?

Do you accept the fact that the Bible's definition of grace— God's unmerited favor shown to people who are totally undeserving of it—applies to you not only in salvation but in your everyday life? The meaning of grace never changes. As I've said, grace is always the same, whether God is exercising it in salvation or in His dealings with us as His children.

Jesus said, "I have come that [you] may have life, and have it to the full" (John 10:10 NIV). Do you have life, that is, eternal life? Have you renounced all confidence in your own moral or religious efforts and turned in faith completely to Jesus to be clothed with *His* righteousness? If so, you do have eternal life. But do you have it to the full? Are you experiencing both the peace of God that comes with salvation and the joy of God that comes with living by grace each day? If not, you may be saved by grace, but you are living by works. ✧

For it is by grace you have been saved, through faith— and this not from yourselves, it is the gift of God— not by works, so that no one can boast.

Ephesians 2:8-9 NIV

✧

Thus all below is strength, and all above is grace.

—John Dryden

32

Broken for You

Paul Brand and Philip Yancey

Repentance does not mean remorse. Repentance means giving up sin.

—W. E. Biederwolf

❧

C. S. Lewis reminds us that repentance "is not something God demands of you before He will take you back and which He could let you off if He chose; it is simply a description of what going back is like." The past hanging thickly over us needs to be remembered in order to be forgotten. Repentance is for our sakes, not to punish us, but to free us from the harmful effects of accumulated sins. "This is His body, broken for you" . . . for your gossiping, your lust, your pride, your insensitivity . . . broken to remove all those and replace them with His perfect obedience.

Why do any of us go to church and sit on rather uncomfortable furniture, in stiff clothes, lined up in rows as in a high school classroom, singing songs unlike any we have heard all week? Is it not because in each of us a spark of hope has been lit—a hope to be known, to be forgiven, to be healed, to be loved? Something like this yearning lies at the heart of the ceremony of the Lord's Supper.

Symbols are weaker than the reality behind them. But Christ has given us the wine and the bread as proof that we are forgiven, healed, and loved. The symbol works its way inside us, becoming material as well as spiritual nourishment, carrying its message to individual cells throughout each body.

In the Eucharist, we are reminded of the overarching forgiveness accomplished in Christ's sacrifice that made obsolete the whole Jewish sacrificial system. "For if, when we were God's enemies, we were reconciled to him through the death of his Son, how much more, having been reconciled, shall we be saved through his life!" (Romans 5:10 NIV). If sin is the great separator, Christ is the Great Reconciler. He dissolves the membrane of separation that grows up every day between ourselves and others, ourselves and God. "Now in Christ Jesus," said Paul elsewhere, "you who once were far away have been brought near through the blood of Christ. For he himself is our peace" (Ephesians 2:13-14 NIV).

Near the end of his life, Francois Mauriac, the French Catholic novelist who received the Nobel Prize for Literature, reflected on his own love-hate history with the church. He detailed the ways in which the church had not kept its promise: the petty way rifts and compromises have always characterized it. The church, he concluded, has strayed far from the precepts and example of its Founder.

And yet, added Mauriac, despite all its failings the church has at least remembered two words of Christ: "Your sins are forgiven you," and "This is my body broken for you." The Lord's Supper brings together those two words in a quiet ceremony of healing by cleansing individual cells in His Body of all impurities. ❧

For I have not come to call the righteous, but sinners.

—Matthew 9:13 NIV

❧

To do it no more is the truest repentance.

—Martin Luther

33

Not Perfect, Just Forgiven

Charles Swindoll

Christians are not perfect, just forgiven.

—Anonymous

&

Non-Christians are stumped when it comes to the grace of God and the humanity of Christians. Why? Because their whole perspective is horizontal. Things that are valuable are costly. Therefore, it is inconceivable that something as priceless as heaven could be offered as a free gift.

There isn't much running loose on the horizontal plane. And since their whole frame of reference is so man-centered, it's virtually impossible for them to imagine an individual who claims he belongs to God and one who still struggles with imperfection. After all, if you say God has come into your life and Christ has wiped your slate clean, how come you aren't perfect?

That's the non-Christian's way of thinking, and I accept that. They equate salvation with perfection—no wonder they're confused! Being fellow members of one another, we understand that becoming a Christian in no way ushers us into a life of perfection, erasing our humanity and eradicating our depravity.

If all that actually happened, then why in the world is the Bible filled with counsel on forgiving others, understanding their failures, and focusing on their strengths? It's one thing for an unbeliever to expect perfection—I can live with that and tolerate it fairly well—but it's most disconcerting to be pushed into a perfection mold by brothers and sisters!

Oh, I understand that our example is Christ . . . and that our standard is high . . . and that our motives are often good. But it needs to be said again and again and again: *Christians are not perfect, just forgiven.*

How quickly the thin thread of freedom snaps as heavy weights of perfectionistic expectations are placed upon us! Christ Jesus never did that with His own. When people were near Him there was this incredible magnetism because of an absence of unrealistic expectations and subtle demands and manipulative devices. He did not use pressure tactics. He simply accepted people as they were.

A paralysis sets in when we operate in the choking context of the perfection-expectation syndrome. Fed by fear and guilt, the Christian becomes a victim of others rather than a victor in Christ. You see, we ultimately act out those pressures and thereby limit our potential.

Let's back off! Let's relax the stranglehold on each others' necks. I love what Ruth Graham once so wisely said: "It's my job to love Billy. It's God's job to make him good." ❧

Be kind and compassionate to one another,
forgiving each other, just as in Christ God forgave you.

Ephesians 4:32 NIV

❧

It is only one step from toleration to forgiveness.
—Sir Arthur Wing Pinero

34

How Will You Respond?

Charles Colson

*Obedience to God is the most infallible evidence of
sincere and supreme love to Him.*

—Nathanael Emmons

During the period of the divided kingdom, Ahab, described as the most corrupt in a long line of corrupt leaders, became king of Israel. And he "considered it trivial to commit the sins of his predecessors" (1 Kings 16:31). This man who angered God more than all the evil kings considered his sins *trivial.*

Ahab was not unique. So powerful is the human tendency to trivialize sin that only the Holy Spirit can open our eyes. As John and other writers of Scripture point out, the Spirit must convict us of our sinful nature.

Without the conviction of the Holy Spirit and the repentance that must follow, there is no way out of our [sinful] predicament. We have the capacity to change anything about our lives— jobs, homes, cars, even spouses—but we cannot change our own sinful nature.

Years after his personal encounter with Christ, the Apostle Paul posed the eternal question: "What a wretched man I am! Who will rescue me from this body of death?" (Romans 7:24 NIV). He saw the moral precepts could not free him; in fact, paradoxically, they made matters worse while convicting him. He said, "I would not have known what it was to covet if the law had not said, 'Do not covet.' But sin, seizing the opportunity afforded by the commandment, produced in me every kind of covetous desire" (Romans 7:7-8).

What a desperate plight. Trapped in and by our own sin. Thankfully, there is an answer to the wrenching dilemma. Paul described it in the next chapter of his letter to the Romans: "There is now no condemnation for those who are in Christ Jesus. . . . For what the law was powerless to do in that it was weakened by the sinful nature, God did by sending his own Son . . . to be a sin offering" (Romans 8:1,3 NIV). That took place that momentous day on Golgotha nearly 2,000 years ago.

And how is all this part of loving God? Well, when we see the reality of our sin, when we come face to face with it and look into the raging fire of hell itself, and when we then repent and believe and are delivered from that plight, our entire being is filled with unspeakable gratitude to the God Who sent His Son to that cross for us.

We must express that gratitude. But how? Simply stated: by living the way He commands. By obedience. That is what the Scripture means by holiness or sanctification—believers are set apart for holy living. Therefore, holiness is the only possible response to God's grace. Holy living is loving God. &

If you love me, you will obey what I command.

—John 14:15 NIV

&

Gratitude is from the same root word as "grace,"
which signifies the free and boundless mercy of God.

—Willis P. King

35

Maturing in Grace

Oswald Chambers

*Grace is free, but when once you take it you are bound
forever to the Giver, and bound to catch the spirit of the Giver.*

—E. Stanley Jones

When we are young in grace we go where we want to go, but a time comes when Jesus says "another shall gird thee" and our will and wish are not asked for. This stage of spiritual experience brings us into fellowship with the Spirit of Jesus, for it is written large over His life that even Christ pleased not Himself.

There is a distinct period in our experience when we cease to say, "Lord, show me Thy will," and the realization begins to dawn that we *are* God's will, and He can do with us what He likes. We wake up to the knowledge that we have the privilege of giving ourselves over to God's will. It is a question of being yielded to God.

When we are young in grace there is a note of independence about our spiritual life: "I don't intend anyone to tell me what to do, I intend to serve God as I choose." It is an independence based on inexperience, an immature fellowship; it lacks the essential of devotion. Some of us remain true to the independent following and never get beyond it; but we are built for God Himself, not for service for God, and that explains the submissions of life. We can easily escape the submissions if we like to rebel against them, but the Spirit of God will produce humiliation if we do not submit.

Since we became disciples of Jesus we cannot be as independent as we used to be, saying, "I do wish Jesus did not expect so much of me." He expects nothing less than absolute oneness with Himself as He was one with the Father. That is the "hope of His calling" (Ephesians 1:18 NKJV) and it is the great light on every problem. Jesus makes us saints in order that we may sacrifice our saintship to Him, and it is this sacrifice which keeps us one with our Lord.

In the natural world it is a real delight to be faced with risk and danger, and in the spiritual world God gives us the "sporting chance." He will plant us down amongst all kinds of people and give us the amazing joy of proving ourselves "a living sacrifice" in those circumstances. The Father's heart was thrilled with delight at the loyalty of His Son. Is Jesus Christ thrilled with delight at the way we are living a sacrificial life of holiness? The disciple has no program, only a distinguished passion of devotion to his Lord. &

But grow in the grace and knowledge of our Lord and Savior Jesus Christ. To him be glory both now and forever! Amen.

—2 Peter 3:18 NIV

&

Grace is but glory begun, and glory is but grace perfected.

—Jonathan Edwards

Power for Living

Spiritual power begins with the surrender of
the individual to God. It commences with
obedience to the first commandment.

—William Jennings Bryant

36

Victorious Surrender

Debra Evans

The essence of true holiness consists in
conformity to the nature and will of God.

— Samuel Lucas

"Come to Me." When the circumstances of life are beyond our ability to bear them, when there seems to be no way for things to work out, when rapids hit and the boat threatens to capsize at any moment, when a sudden change in life plans cancels our dreams and reroutes the future, Jesus stands before us, and with His arms opened wide, extends this incredible invitation. Surrendering our burdens at His feet and placing each heavy parcel before the cross, we can choose to close our ears to competing commands and confusing directions, and listen for God's voice alone.

Surrender never discounts or denies the reality of our suffering. When Jesus agonizingly prayed in the Garden of Gethsemane, "Father, if you are willing, take this cup from me; yet not my will but yours be done" (Luke 22:42 NIV), there can be no doubt that He knew what was at stake in the battle looming ahead. Quietly facing His accusers, He submitted to their authority, fully recognizing the costs involved. He understood what the terms of His surrender would be.

But that is not all: By laying down His life before His enemies in obedience to God's will, Jesus demolished the opposition.

Through surrender—bowing before God's mighty throne, laying each struggle before our Father in heaven, casting out all grief and heartache, giving up to Jesus every source of suffering and sin—we participate, with Christ, in His kingdom's victories. We cannot do it on our own. We are not supposed to even try to do it on our own. Heeding the Lord's command to surrender, we are continually surprised to find that, somehow, in a way that is totally beyond our comprehension, *He triumphs through us.*

"Holiness in us is the copy or transcript of the holiness that is in Christ," believed Philip Henry. "As the wax hath line for line from the seal, and the child feature for feature from the Father, so is holiness also from Him." Do you believe that the beauty of holiness is God's promised gift to "ordinary" people instead of something that only a few outstanding saints achieve?

Take heart, then. Pray for the grace of surrender. Receive all of the peace, and joy, and love that Jesus freely offers. He is waiting. His arms are open. What He has done for the greatest saints, He surely can do for you and me. ❧

Come to me, all you who are weary and burdened,
and I will give you rest. Take my yoke upon you and
learn from me, for I am gentle and humble in heart,
and you will find rest for your souls.

—Matthew 11:28-29 NIV

❧

Suffering accepted and vanquished . . . will give you a serenity
which may well prove the most exquisite fruit of your life.

—Cardinal Mercier

37
Treasure in a Vessel

Watchman Nee

Come, Holy Ghost, our souls inspire,
and lighten with celestial fire.

—Archbishop of Mainz

I could shout with joy as I think, *The Spirit Who dwells within me is no mere influence, but a living Person; He is very God. The infinite God is within my heart!* Oh, my friends, I would fain repeat it to you a hundred times. I am only an earthen vessel, but in that earthen vessel I carry a treasure of unspeakable worth, even the Lord of glory.

All the worry and fret of God's children would end if their eyes were opened to see the greatness of the treasure hid in their hearts. Do you know there are resources enough in your own heart to meet the demand of every circumstance in which you will ever find yourself? Do you know there is power enough to move the city in which you live? Do you know there is power enough to shake the universe? Let me tell you once more—I say it with the utmost reverence: You who have been born again of the Spirit of God—you carry God in your heart!

Do you realize what happened at your conversion? God came into your heart and made it His temple. In Solomon's days God dwelt in a temple made of stone: today He dwells in a temple composed of living believers. When we really see that God has made our hearts His dwelling place, what a deep reverence will come over our lives! Has it really come home to you that wherever you go you carry with you the Holy Spirit of God? You do not just carry your Bible with you, or even much good teaching about God, but God Himself.

The reason why many Christians do not experience the power of the Spirit, though He actually dwells in their hearts, is that they lack reverence. And they lack reverence because they have not had their eyes opened to the fact of His presence. The fact is there, but they have not seen it.

Why is it that some of God's children live victorious lives while others are in a state of constant defeat? The difference is not accounted for by the presence or absence of the Spirit (for He dwells in the heart of every child of God) but by this, that some recognize His indwelling and others do not. True revelation of the fact of the Spirit's indwelling will revolutionize the life of any Christian.

The difference between victorious Christians and defeated ones is not that some have the Spirit while others have not, but that some know His indwelling and others do not, and consequently some recognize the divine ownership of their lives while others are still their own masters.

Revelation is the first step to holiness, and consecration is the second. A day comes in our lives, as definite as the day of our conversion, when we give up all right to ourselves and submit to the absolute Lordship of Jesus Christ. ❧

Be filled with the Spirit.

—Ephesians 5:18 NIV

❧

We must not be content to be cleansed from sin;
we must be filled with the Spirit.

—John Fletcher

38

Overcoming the World

Mark I. Bubeck

Be wisely worldly, but not worldly wise.

— Francis Quarles

The believer can handle the world's temptations and walk before God in victory over the world. It is certain that we must remain a part of the world system until our Lord calls us home to heaven. Our victory over the world is ours to claim while we live it here and now.

We can have victory through our faith. "For whatsoever is born of God overcometh the world: and this is the victory that overcometh the world, even our faith. Who is he that overcometh the world, but he that believeth that Jesus is the Son of God" (1 John 5:4-5 KJV).

John defines the believer's victory over the world as "our faith." In a general sense, our faith includes the whole body of revealed truth which has come to us by the revelation of God. Our faith overcomes the world in this sense by the inner assimilation of God's revealed Word. As the believer becomes grounded in the faith through his understanding of God's Word, all worldly values are measured and overcome by the truth of the Word.

There is more personal application of the victory of our faith over the world, however, and this comes to us through our union with the Lord Jesus Christ. First John 5:5 states that our overcoming is through believing that Jesus is the Son of God.

In John 16:33 the Lord Jesus declared, "These things I have spoken unto you, that in me ye might have peace. In the world ye shall have tribulation: but be of good cheer; I have overcome the world" (KJV). This verse declares that the hope the disciples have of victory over the tribulations of the world is that Christ has overcome the world.

As by faith believers enter into His victory over the world, they, too, shall overcome and defeat the world. This is why it is good to claim the perfect, sinless victorious life Christ lived as a human being on this earth as your daily victory. The deceptions of Satan through the world system are very subtle. As we claim our victory in the Lord Jesus Christ, it is His life that secures our victory. He is able to deliver us from this present evil world. He is able to "succor us," or to help us right now when the world tempts us. Because Christ is crucified to the world, so am I.

What comfort and assurance there is for the believer who sees how totally our Lord Jesus Christ defeated the world and Satan who rules over the world system. Our victory is through the One Who is in us. "Ye are of God, little children, and have overcome them: because greater is he that is in you, than he that is in the world" (1 John 4:4 KJV).

I have told you these things, so that in me you may have peace.
In this world you will have trouble. But take heart!
I have overcome the world.

—John 16:33 NIV

The early Christians not only moved the world;
they turned it upside down.

—George Jackson

39

The Authority of Heaven

Stuart Briscoe

God of the present age and hour,
thrill us anew with holy power!

—William Stewart Gordon

One time a group of us decided that a large construction that had stood on the grounds of Capernwray Hall since the war ought to be removed. But it was made of solid concrete. Picks, hammers, and chisels would make no impression. Honest sweat and bulging muscles were useless. The concrete could resist every attack upon it—except one—dynamite!

There is something virile about the words *dynamite* and *dynamic.* The very sound of the words suggests action, movement, and irresistible power. *Dunamis* is the Greek word from which these words derive, and in the New Testament *dunamis* is translated "power." Make no mistake: it will take this kind of explosive to get the hard core of evil splintered with the Gospel in these days.

You may have been surprised to hear that we used dynamite to move our concrete slab. However, we obtained the necessary permission first. There was nothing illegal about our actions, for we were fully authorized to act in that way.

The Lord said, "All authority has been given to Me in heaven and on earth" (Matthew 28:18 NKJV). Then He said that He would be with us. If all authority is His and He is with His people, they have all His authority—authority that is valid in heaven and on earth. The Lord also added, "You shall receive power when the Holy Spirit has come upon you" (Acts 1:8 NKJV).

This is the position of strength for a Christian. We have the authority of heaven behind us and the dynamic of heaven within us. When we recognize our rightful authority, we are confident and don't have to go around trying to prove ourselves. Our authority is obvious. If we have the corresponding power, we are [dangerous and] a force to be reckoned with.

Dangerous Christians don't only create danger; they attract it. The crack marksman on the field of battle will always be a prime target for the enemy. The star athlete on the football field always draws the heaviest tackling. The Christian who rejoices in the all-sufficient power of the Spirit of God within draws the biggest temptation and the greatest opposition. That is why some Christians don't want to be dangerous, and they turn down the opportunity for God's kind of adventure. They prefer to be comfortable.

We live in exciting days. There is much to be done, great victories to be won. Will you settle for anything other than the fullness of the grace of God in your life that will make you able to handle all that comes your way? &

Then Jesus came to them and said,
"All authority in heaven and on earth has been given to me."
—Matthew 28:18 NIV

&

The devil and me we don't agree, glory hallelujah!
I hate him and he hates me, glory hallelujah!
—Salvation Army Chorus

40

The Name of Jesus

Quin Sherrer and Ruthanne Garlock

All hail the power of Jesus' name!

—Edward Perronet

Our conflict is with an invisible enemy and his evil agents in the spiritual realm, who operate through individuals. We cannot use physical weapons against enemy agents, but God has given us invisible spiritual weapons. [One of our primary weapons is] the name of Jesus. Consider these Scriptures:

"You are my King and my God . . . Through you we push back our enemies; through your name we trample our foes. I do not trust in my bow, my sword does not bring me victory; but you give us victory over our enemies, you put our adversaries to shame" (Psalm 44:4-7 NIV).

"The seventy-two returned with joy, and said, 'Lord, even the demons submit to us in your name.' He replied, ' . . . I have given you authority to trample on snakes and scorpions and to overcome all the power of the enemy; nothing will harm you'" (Luke 10:17-19 NIV).

"They overcame him [Satan] by the blood of the Lamb and by the word of their testimony" (Revelation 12:11 NIV).

The only way to use the name of Jesus as a weapon is to speak to the enemy. Jesus spoke to Satan in the wilderness; He also spoke to a fig tree and cursed it. So don't feel reticent about speaking to the evil powers of darkness. Paul Billheimer says, "The only way we can be sure that he [Satan] knows we are resisting him is to speak aloud, to directly and audibly confront him with the truth. May I remind you that *our resistance* by itself is not what causes Satan to flee; he flees because of the *power of Jesus* which is ours through prayer."

Bible teacher Dean Sherman expands on this thought: "Man . . . has authority, based on what Christ did on the cross and His resurrection. Man can still employ Satan through selfishness and sin, but the balance of power on the earth rests with man in the name of Jesus Christ. The authority is complete in man as long as man is in relationship with God through Jesus Christ.

"With our authority comes the responsibility to use it for God's purposes. If we don't rebuke the devil, he will not be rebuked. If we don't drive him back, he will not leave. It is up to us. Satan knows of our authority, but hopes we will stay ignorant. We must be as convinced of our authority as the devil is."

The sacrificial death, burial, and resurrection of Jesus is the basis of our victory over Satan. He is the sinless sacrifice, the "Lamb that was slain from the creation of the world" (Revelation 13:8 NIV). When we confess our sins and repent (meaning to turn from sin), the blood of Jesus cleanses us and puts us in right relationship with God. When we have this experience, we are not only protected by the blood of Jesus; we are authorized to use the blood as a weapon of warfare. ❧

That at the name of Jesus every knee should bow.

Philippians 2:10 NIV

❧

Jesus! The name high over all . . . Angels and men
before it fall, and devils fear and fly.

—Charles Wesley

41

Our Victory

F. J. Huegel

Renounce the devil and all his works.

— Book of Common Prayer

Jesus not only came to reveal the Father's love, to express in terms of human life the divine purpose; He not only came to heal and to teach; it was not simply to give His life as a ransom for many there upon the cross. There was one supreme purpose of which little was said because man in his blindness would not understand.

Behind the scenes there was being enacted a mighty drama. Jesus saw Satan fall as lightning from heaven. He saw the real enemy. Not for a second was He deceived. Men were under the dominion of the powers of darkness. The master's supreme glory, His prime value as Redeemer, lay in the fact that He was able to break the power. He cast out demons. He faced the enemy in the desert and came forth victor.

But is not God omnipotent? Why could He not with one strike have upset the whole Satanic hierarchy? He could have, but that would not have answered His purpose, not solved the problem. Man had sinned. Man had been deceived by the father of lies. Man had made common cause with Satan. So it was necessary that man of his own free will should break with Satan and return to the Father. Christ as man overcame Satan. Herein lies the virtue of it all. It was the Son of Man employing weapons which man might use, *triumphing*.

But to come to the point of interest for us. What has all this to do with participation? Much, every way. We are not only baptized unto Christ's death, and raised with Him in the power of an endless life; we are the participants of His victory over the forces of hell. When the Son of Man achieved, we potentially achieved in Him. The humblest believer may trample the "dragon" under foot. The weakest disciple who realizes his oneness with Christ, may in His name "bind the strong man" and spoil him of his goods.

The humblest believer who realizes his oneness with Christ is invested with the very authority of the Son of God. Shall we not judge angels? As members of His body we share His executive authority. If God be for us who can be against us? Yea, verily! Mountains do move and are cast into the sea at our bidding. The apostles exercised this power and we may exercise it.

Christ stands ready to make effective the command of the humblest lamb of His flock, if that lamb is obedient. But we cannot have all that Christ has for us in this regard until He has all of us. God grant us a disposition to die with Christ that with Him we may reign. ❧

This is love for God: to obey his commands.
And his commands are not burdensome,
for everyone born of God overcomes the world.
This is the victory that has overcome the world, even our faith.

—1 John 5:3-4 NIV

❧

Every evil comes to us on wings and goes away limping.

—French Proverb

42

Strength Is for Service

Barbara Cook

Nothing is so strong as gentleness; nothing so gentle as real strength.

—St. Francis de Sales

Jesus had great power, but He chose to see Himself as a servant. He told His followers, "For even the Son of Man did not come to be served, but to serve, and to give his life as a ransom for many" (Mark 10:45 NIV). That was His life's purpose, and He lived out that purpose daily.

[Yet] Jesus was not a victim. He *chose*. He was not used, manipulated, coerced, or trapped at any point, even in His death. In His discourse on the good shepherd He said, "No one takes it [my life] from me, but I lay it down of my own accord" (John 10:18 NIV).

As Christians, we no longer need to live powerlessly. Being a victim is not part of the new life Christ has given us. Why can we say that so confidently? Because Paul's epistle to the Romans deals with that very issue. Romans tells us that powerlessness and the helplessness syndrome was B.C. [before Christ]. It's in the past.

"You see, at just the right time, when we were still powerless, Christ died for the ungodly" (Romans 5:6 NIV).

We used to be powerless. But no more. Christ has solved that problem. Romans 5 makes this announcement: "How much more will those who receive God's abundant provision of grace . . . reign in life through . . . Jesus Christ" (verse 17 NIV). A person who reigns in life is not a victim—unless he or she allows it. A person who reigns in life never says, "I had no choice. There was nothing I could do."

If we are reigning, we are making choices. With the power of the Holy Spirit inside us, those choices can be made confidently.

When we choose to use the talents, intelligence, and power God has entrusted to us, we do so not to appease expectations; to get someone off our back; or even worse, to coerce, exploit, and damage others, but to bless them.

This is a more genuine serving than that dutiful drudgery put out by the victim. When we, as free agents—strong, valuable, and empowered by God—cheerfully offer our service to others, it is a true choice. Our service is a gift. No mixed motives. No waiting like the obedient puppy for a pat on the head and a few table scraps.

We love because it is our nature to love. We choose loving service as the best way to live our lives. Living a life of love is the wise choice of a person who has accepted God-given power. &

Blessed are those whose strength is in you.

—Psalm 84:5 NIV

&

The world cannot always understand one's profession of faith, but it can understand service.

—Ian Maclaren

SECTION SEVEN

Gifts of Guidance

Lord, through this hour, be Thou our Guide,
so by Thy power, no foot shall slide.

—Westminster Chimes

43

God's Mysterious Guidance

Paul Tournier

*Providence has at all times been my only dependence,
for all other resources seem to have failed us.*

—George Washington

God guides us, despite our uncertainties and vagueness, even through our failings and mistakes. He often starts us off to the left, only to bring us up in the end to the right; or else He brings us back to the right, after a long detour, because we started off by mistake to the left in the belief that we were obeying Him.

He leads us step by step, from event to event. Only afterwards, as we look back over the way we have come and reconsider certain important moments in our lives in the light of all that has followed them, or when we survey the whole progress of our lives, do we experience the feeling of having been led without knowing it, the feeling that God has mysteriously guided us.

It was He Who made us meet this man, made us hear that remark, read that book, with all the decisive consequences they have had on our lives. We did not perhaps know it at the time. Time has had to elapse to enable us to see it. Thus, the disciples on the Emmaus road talked with Jesus without recognizing Him. It was He Who brought us up short by means of a dream which at first we did not understand, a serious illness, a strange hesitation, or a painful failure. It was He also Who guided us by means of a success, and so opened up a new and unexpected horizon to us. Ah, that is the true answer to our perplexing problem of success and failure!

God has a purpose: the entire Bible proclaims this. What matters is that His plan should be understood and fulfilled. So, in the light of the Bible the problem is shifted on to a new ground. The question is no longer whether one is succeeding or failing, but whether one is fulfilling God's purpose or not, whether one is adventuring with Him or against Him.

It is, of course, always a joyful thing to succeed. But the joy is very deceptive if it comes from the satisfaction of an ambition that is contrary to the will of God. And of course failure is still very painful; but the pain is fruitful if it is part of God's purpose. A failure, within God's purpose, is no longer really a failure. Then the Cross, the supreme failure, is at the same time the supreme triumph of God, since it is the accomplishment of the purpose of salvation. This is the true answer to the painful discovery that it is not possible to establish a clear frontier between success and failure.

What is success and what is failure? The answer of the Bible is, "What is the will of God? Are you obeying Him?" ❧

For this God is our God for ever and ever;
he will be our guide even to the end.

—Psalm 48:14 NIV

❧

To have faith where you cannot see; to be
willing to work on in the dark; to be conscious
of the fact that, so long as you strive for the best,
there are better things on the way, this in itself is success.

—Katherine Logan

44

Everyday Guidance

Paul Brand and Philip Yancey

*I find the doing of the will of God leaves me
no time for disputing about His plans.*

— George Macdonald

Quite often I meet Christians who tend to wear their spirituality as an aura of otherworldliness. According to some, the most spiritual Christian is one who confidently asserts, "God told me it's time to buy a new dress," or, "I'm positive God wants our church to use our money this way." "God told me" can become a casual manner of speech.

Actually, I believe most of what God has to say to me is already written in the Bible and the onus is on me to diligently study His will revealed there. For most of us, mysterious, direct messages from a hotline to God are not the ordinary ways of discerning His will. Guidance mediated through circumstances or modified on the advice of wise Christian friends, though it may seem less spectacular, is not at all inferior.

College graduates agonize over what decisions to make for the future, waiting for God to alert them with a jolting, custom-made plan dropped into their laps. In the Bible God indeed employed the supernatural means of angels and visions and the like to convey His will. But, if you look closely at those incidents, you will note that few of them came in response to a prayer for guidance. They were usually unrequested and unexpected.

Consider the oft-cited Macedonian call of Paul as an example. Spectacular, yes, since a vision of a man beckoned Paul to change his travel plans and head toward Macedonia. Note carefully, however, that the vision prompted Paul to *change* his plans. You would expect Paul to plan his future in a godly way, but this incident indicates that Paul had gone off on his missionary journey without any visions or inner voices from the Spirit. Most likely, he looked over the situation and chose the route that seemed the most sensible. But the Holy Spirit wanted him to go into a whole new region—and so intervened spectacularly. It was exceptional guidance, obviously not the kind Paul normally relied on.

When grasping for analogies to describe the growth in faith of the individual believer, Paul often turned to athletics: running, boxing, wrestling. Athletes demonstrate well the discipline that can train the body toward predictable, dependable actions. And an athlete's body knows what his mind wants and is equipped and experienced to effect that desire. Similarly, the individual Christian would better spend his time working on practical, daily obedience to what God has already revealed rather than fervent searches for some magic secret, elusive as the Holy Grail. &

Show me your ways, O LORD, teach me your paths; guide me in your truth and teach me, for you are God my Savior, and my hope is in you all day long.
—Psalm 25:4-5 NIV

&

Henceforth I learn that to obey is best.
—John Milton

45

A Charter for Divine Guidance

Pat Robertson

*An undivided heart, which worships God alone, and trusts
Him as it should, is raised above all anxiety for earthly wants.*

—John Cunningham Geikie

"Trust in the LORD with all thine heart; and lean not unto thine own understanding. In all thy ways acknowledge him, and he shall direct thy paths" (Proverbs 3:5-6 KJV).

This is certainly a charter for divine guidance. This Scripture is His promise to us. However, this promise is conditioned on certain things, and I think you need to understand the conditions.

Trust in the Lord with all your heart. Your heart is the innermost part of you, the citadel of your personality, the core and motivation of your being. It is the deepest part of your spiritual life, the part that makes everything else tick— and that part of you must be centered totally on God.

David put it another way when he said, "My heart is fixed, O God" (Psalm 57:7 KJV). If a ship is being guided by a directional instrument, that instrument must be fixed on a course, or the ship will be plowing through the sea in an aimless fashion. The guidance system of that ship must be fixed.

It will do you no good to have your heart fixed on personal wealth or other selfish motives, while at the same time you claim to have fixed it on God. Your heart must be zeroed in on one target—God Almighty—and the relationship must be one of absolute trust.

The second rule of divine guidance is: *Do not lean on your own understanding.* If, while I was following a compass course, I began to follow a beautiful road that wandered off my course, I would miss my destination. The same thing is true of divine guidance. You cannot lean on your own understanding. Neither you nor I has any knowledge of the future. We cannot, with any degree of certainty, say what will happen to us, to our surroundings, or to our world. Only God knows.

The third principle of divine guidance is: *In all your ways acknowledge Him.* You cannot expect God to guide you in the issues that you regard as important, while at the same time you ignore Him in the little things. If you are not faithful in what is least, you will not be faithful in what is great. But if you are faithful in the little things in your life, then the Word of God says that you will be faithful in the great things.

Three necessary steps, and He shall direct your paths. He shall give you direction. ❧

Those who know your name will trust in you, for you,
LORD, have never forsaken those who seek you.

—Psalm 9:10 NIV

❧

God provides for him that trusteth.

—George Herbert

46

Hearing His Voice

Martha Thatcher

Nothing is of faith that is not in Scripture.

— Benjamin Whichcote

There are basically two arenas in which we listen to God. One is the quiet, private times with God in His Word. As Christians, we do well to develop patterns and habits that keep us available to God in His Word. We also must pray concerning our focus in those times and think about helpful ways to keep our eyes on God as we examine His Word.

As we know God more intimately, we will hear His voice more clearly, more specifically, more frequently. A. W. Tozer has written, "I think a new world will arise out of the religious mists when we approach our Bible with the idea that it is not only a book which was once spoken, but a book which is *now speaking.*"

The second arena in which we hear the voice of God is out in our "field." Much of what happens in our lives is God's non-verbal communication with us. Do we find ourselves thrown about by a series of unexpected events? Perhaps God is saying, "Trust Me." Are we hurt and disappointed that plans or relationships haven't materialized in the way we had hoped? It may be that God is telling us that He alone is our security. Have we watched people's lives turn about as they choose to obey God? Maybe He is helping us observe how pleased He is with obedience.

Perhaps we have a friend who faithfully advises us when we lose our objectivity. Or an acquaintance who criticizes us. Maybe we are just listening as someone tells about his spiritual journey, or how God dealt with him in a certain situation. In all these circumstances and many others, we find ourselves out in the "field" surrounded by voices, noise, and activity. If we have trained our ears to hear God, we will recognize His voice even in the most unlikely places.

Any voice we recognize as God's in the field of life must be the same voice we hear in the Bible. If we haven't cultivated our familiarity with God's powerfully comforting voice behind closed doors, we are in danger of mistaking many field voices as God's. Much of what we hear, even in our Christian circles, sounds good, but it does not come from God. Or, even though it reflects God's truth, it may not be God's timely instruction for *us*. We can tie ourselves in knots when, because we do not hear *God*, we try to follow all the right-sounding voices, all the ones that claim God's direction.

Our ability to hear God's voice is a gift from Him that must be cultivated in private with a focus on God in His Word, and practiced everywhere. ❧

But my eyes are fixed on you, O Sovereign LORD;
in you I take refuge.

—Psalm 141:8 NIV

❧

I believe in God as I believe in my friends because I feel
the breath of His affection, feel His invisible and
tangible hand drawing me, leading me, grasping me.

—Miguel de Unamuno

47

Believing the Call

Elisabeth Elliot

God gives man a will, but he must make the right choices.

— Bishop Fulton J. Sheen

We need never ask the question, "How do I know I'm called?" We ought rather to ask, "How do I know I am *not* called?" We are required to take the risk, move, trust God, make a beginning.

This is what Jesus always asked of those who came to Him for help of any kind. Sometimes He asked them to state their case ("What do you want Me to do?"), to affirm their desire ("Do you want to be healed?"), and often to do something positive ("Stretch out your hand") before He could do His work. There had to be evidence of faith, some kind of beginning on their part.

The first baby step of faith is followed by a daily walk of obedience, and it is as we continue with Him in His Word that we are assured that we were, in fact, called and have nothing to fear. The commonest fear of the true disciple, I suppose, is his own unworthiness. When Paul wrote to the Corinthians, a group of Christians who had made some terrible messes even inside the church itself, he still never doubted their calling; for they were prepared to hear the Word and to be guided and corrected.

It was not the *perfection* of their faith that convinced him they were called. They had made a beginning. In that beginning, Paul found evidence of faith: "It is in full reliance upon God, through Christ, that we make such claims. There is no question of our being qualified in ourselves: we cannot claim anything on our own. The qualification we have comes from God" (2 Corinthians 3:4-5).

Young people sometimes say to me, "I'll just die if the Lord calls me to be a missionary," or words to that effect.

"Wonderful!" I say. "That's the best possible way to start. You won't be of much use on the mission field unless you 'die' first." The conditions for discipleship begin with "dying," and if you take the first step, very likely you will find that you have indeed been "called."

Desire and conviction both play a part in vocation. Often the desire comes first. There may be a natural inclination or an interest aroused by information or perhaps an unexplained longing. If these sometimes deceptive feelings are offered to the Master and subjected to the test of His Word, they will be confirmed by various means and become a conviction. The only thing to do then is to arise and go.

The believer alone will be able to hear the call. It comes from beyond ourselves, beyond our society, beyond the climate of opinion and prejudices and rebellion and skepticism in which we live, beyond our time and taste. &

With this in mind, we constantly pray for you, that our God may count you worthy of his calling, and that by his power he may fulfill every good purpose of yours and every act prompted by your faith.

—2 Thessalonians 1:11 NIV

&

Nothing is really lost by a life of sacrifice; everything is lost by failure to obey God's call.

—Henry Parry Liddon

48

Knowing God's Will

Ingrid Trobisch

All work that is worth anything is done in faith.

—Albert Schweitzer

❧

"But how can we hear the voice of the gentle Shepherd?" you ask. [My husband] Walter once wrote a letter to his friends about how we can know God's will. Here is the gist of what he said.

1. Often guidance will become clear when we take a concrete step in a certain direction. All at once a still, small voice speaks to us gently in our hearts and we know, "I am going in the right direction," or, "This step is wrong." According to 1 Kings 19:12, the Lord was not in the strong wind or the earthquake or the fire—all very dramatic occurrences. He spoke in a sound of gentle stillness. The sound cannot be heard from the outside. Only those who have inner antennae and who stop and listen in their quiet time will be able to know God's guidance.

2. If the inner antennae have received the message, then you must follow it through without looking to the left or right, without paying attention to the way the wind blows. "He who observes the wind [and waits on all conditions to be favorable] will not sow; and he who regards the clouds will not reap" (Ecclesiastes 11:4 RSV). The outward circumstances are always ambiguous and can only be interpreted correctly in the light of the still, small voice. This sign, which is outside our control, is infallible.

It is like the needle of a compass that shows us the direction we should take, or like the directions given from the control tower when a plane is landing. We can hear a small voice telling us, "This is not right for you. Hands off!" Or we hear, "This is a good opportunity for you. Try it."

3. The art of letting oneself be guided also includes the readiness to be corrected. It is humiliating to admit before God, before oneself, and before others, "I made a mistake, I was wrong." Significantly enough, in Psalm 119 we read twice about humiliation. This is Martin Luther's translation, "Before I was afflicted [humiliated], I went astray" (verse 67). "It was good for me that I was afflicted [humiliated] that I might learn thy statutes" (verse 71). To accept humiliation is part of the learning process in the art of finding God's guidance.

To perceive and then to decide—God does not show us the whole way but only the next step. His promise is, "I will counsel you with my eye upon you" (Psalm 32:8 RSV). &

He guides me in paths of righteousness for his name's sake.

—Psalm 23:3 NIV

&

To believe in something not yet proved and to underwrite it with our lives: it is the only way we can keep the future open.

—Lillian Smith

49
Look Up and Follow

Corrie ten Boom

The cross is "I" crossed out.

—Anonymous

A paratroop instructor said that there are four commands he gives his parachutists: *Attention! Stand in the door! Look up! Follow me!* Then the men have to jump.

Jesus is preparing men and women for the new heaven and the new earth and has given His co-workers the same orders the parachutists receive.

Attention! Some people do not believe that there are souls to be saved for eternity. They think everyone will be saved as a matter of course. They need to hear the bad news before the glad news has any value. If we love people we must tell them of the danger of a lost eternity.

Stand in the door! In my travels throughout the world I have often visited mission fields and what a joy it has been to be used by God for the strengthening of missionaries. But there are far more women than men in this work for the Lord. I think there must have been some young men who, when surrendering their lives to Jesus Christ, prayed, "Here I am, Lord, but do send my sister."

"Stand in the door" means that we must be obedient and go where God tells us, whether it be a call to the mission field or a call to work for Him at home. He can use us only when we are in the place where He wants us to be. We dare not keep the gospel a secret but must herald His story forth to all.

Look up! When we look at ourselves we feel unable to be used by the Lord, but when we look to Jesus we become His mirrors. It is true that by itself a mirror does not do much; but when it is hung or placed in the right position it does its job properly. It is very important, therefore, that we should be in the right position. And that position, for a Christian, is "looking unto Jesus the author and finisher of our faith" (Hebrews 12:2 KJV), for we have no light by ourselves.

Follow me! Denying ourselves, taking up our crosses and following Jesus is not like jumping from an airplane toward earth with parachutes on our backs. It means being safe in the hands of Jesus, yoke-bearers with Him. His joy in us and our joy fulfilled.

When we trust ourselves we are doing the wrong thing. We can fall into the error of spiritual pride on the one hand or discouragement on the other. We are really strong when we are weak; weak when we are strong. So following in the footsteps of Jesus, taking the steps—yes, and the jumps into the unknown—we can become paratroopers. We can storm the enemy's territory and win souls for Jesus. &

*Then he called the crowd to him along with his disciples and said:
"If anyone would come after me, he must deny himself and take up
his cross and follow me. For whoever wants to save his life will lose it,
but whoever loses his life for me and for the gospel will save it.
What good is it for a man to gain the whole world, yet forfeit his soul?"*

—Mark 8:34-36 NIV

&

We believe the task ahead of us is never as great as the Power behind us.

—Anonymous

A Certain Hope

We are never beneath hope, while above hell;
nor above hope, while beneath heaven.

—Anonymous

50
The Gift of Hope

Joni Eareckson Tada

The word which God has written on every brow is hope.

—Victor Hugo

"Why are you downcast, O my soul? Why so disturbed within me? Put your hope in God, for I will yet praise him, my Savior and my God" (Psalm 42:5 NIV).

Have you ever started out your day feeling downhearted, a little blue . . . for absolutely no reason? The psalmist asks a good question, "Why are you downcast, O my soul?"

Is it the weather? Is it what you ate last night for supper? Is it an annoyance that's been building, or just a vague, hazy dullness of soul that can't be explained? Often there's simply no reason for being downhearted.

That's why the psalmist quickly advised to put our hope in God and to do it by praising Him. Nothing lifts our spirits quicker or higher than to place our praise at the feet of the Lord Jesus. Why don't you do that right now by saying from your heart (or singing, if you know it) this familiar hymn of praise?

> Though Satan should buffet, tho' trials should come,
> Lest this blest assurance control;
> That Christ has regarded my helpless estate,
> And hath shed His own blood for my soul.

It is well, it is well with my soul.
It is well, it is well with my soul.
And, Lord haste the day when my faith shall be sight,
The clouds be rolled back as a scroll:
The trump shall resound and the Lord shall descend,
"Even so"—it is well with my soul.*

Lord of Hope, I place my trust in You and I praise You for making all things well with my soul. Please receive glory as I magnify and adore Your name, lifting my soul before You. With You, there is no reason to be downhearted.

Be joyful in hope, patient in affliction, faithful in prayer.

—Romans 12:12 NIV

Hope is the parent of faith.

Cyrus Augustus Bartol

---

* Spafford, Horatio O. *The Hymnal for Worship and Celebration*, Word Music, 1986, p. 493.

51

My Hope Is in Thee

Amy Carmichael

When you say a situation or a person is hopeless,
you are slamming the door in the face of God.

—Charles L. Allen

And now, Lord what wait I for? My hope is in Thee. The shadows of evening are stretched out. The clouds are heavy on the mountains. Thou touchest the hills and they smoke.

But like all the clouds of all my life, these heavy clouds are edged with light; and when I look up to the highest cloud I see there no darkness at all, but light, and light beyond light shining down on the peaceful water.

And the water—for I have said to Thee, "Bid me come unto Thee on the water," and Thou has said, "Come"—that water is a pathway of light.

I see a narrow break in the brightness because of the cloud overhead, but soon it is bright again, and then there is no more shadow. And far, far, all but lost in light, I see what I think are other hills, the hills of a better country, even a heavenly.

One evening, as we sat at the end of India on the rocks of Cape Comorin, a little fishing boat sailed into the sunset. It was only a rough thing made of three logs tied together, and its sail was a mere rag, but it was transfigured. To see it was like seeing the mortal put on immortality, the temporal take on the beauty of the eternal.

Usually, I think, a speck of earth entangled in such glory would dare show against the glory, but that evening, so mighty was the power of the golden air, that all of earth was swallowed up. It held us speechless. As I think of it I hear again the lapping of the waves that filled the solace and see the lighted waters in the after-glow.

But what we call sunset the heavenly people call sunrise, and the joy of the Lord, and the morning of God. ◈

Be strong and take heart, all you who hope in the LORD.

—Psalm 31:24

◈

Hope never spread her golden wings
but in unfathomable seas.

—Ralph Waldo Emerson

52
Hope as Big as God

Robert A. Schuller

Hope against hope, and ask till you receive.

—James Montgomery

A man fell off the cliff, caught a branch, and screamed for help. A voice from above told him, "I am your God. I can help you if you let go."

The man replied, "Is there anybody else up there?"

It's an old story that's usually good for a laugh because we all identify with how that man felt. We face situations in which we aren't sure that the God up there can really help us, and wonder if anybody else is available.

[But] have you ever stopped to think about how big God is? The Scriptures tell us that God created the heavens and the earth. How big are the heavens and the earth? It is 240,000 miles from the earth to the moon, yet that's a mere fraction of the distance between the earth and Mars. Then think of the space between Mars and Pluto, which is millions of miles still farther out.

Even with our "tiny" solar system, our distances are almost beyond comprehension. And yet we are but one of many solar systems within the Milky Way. And the Milky Way is one of billions of other galaxies.

It is beyond the capacity of the human mind to understand how big, how vast, how glorious, how grand, and how beautiful God is. And yet from His grandeur, magnificence, and size, God comes to touch the heart of any person who turns to Him in faith.

And with all of His splendor and grandeur, God is also a God of details. Scripture tells us He knows the number of hairs on our heads. He cares for the lilies of the field and for every sparrow, yet He cares for us much more than that. God is interested in the details of your life. He knows exactly where you are at this moment and He knows every problem you face. He knows your frustrations. He knows when you are hoping against hope.

One of my favorite verses says, "No temptation has come your way that is too hard for flesh and blood to bear. But God can be trusted not to allow you to suffer any temptation beyond your powers of endurance. He will see to it that every temptation has its way out, so that it will be possible for you to bear it" (1 Corinthians 10:13).

Dare to believe that God does love you. Believe it against all odds. Dream against all dreams that God does care about you and has a plan for your life and wants you to succeed. Look to God when the reports are bad, when there appears to be no hope. And as you hope against hope, God will hear your prayers. ❧

May the God of hope fill you with all joy and peace
as you trust in him, so that you may overflow with
hope by the power of the Holy Spirit.

—Romans 15:13 NIV

❧

No affliction or temptation, no guilt nor power of sin,
no wounded spirit nor terrified conscience,
should induce us to despair of help and comfort from God.

—Thomas Scott

53

The Reality of Hope

Norman Vincent Peale

Everything that is done in the world is done by hope.

—Martin Luther

What lies behind your ability to fight your way through periods of discouragement or depression? What makes you believe that sooner or later bad times will get better?

It's a little four-letter word that has enormous power in it. Power to bring failures back to success. Power to bring the sick back to health. Power to bring the weak back to strength. It's the word called *hope*.

Saint Paul knew how powerful hope is. He put it right up alongside faith and love as the three great words with power in them.

There's something about hope that makes clear thinking possible. When you're faced with a problem do you regard it with hope or with despondency? If you hope there is a solution, if you believe that somewhere there's a solution, you are probably going to find it. If you think dismally about it, you're likely to come up with dismal results.

We should never write off anything as impossible or as a failure. God gave us the capacity to think our way through any problem. The hopeful thinker projects hope and faith into the darkest situation and lights it up. As long as the thought of defeat is kept out of a person's mind, victory is certain to come sooner or later.

Is there a difference between hoping and wishing? Yes, there is. Hope has the quality of expectancy in it. When you hope strongly, something in you *expects* to have that hope realized. And this tangible called expectancy can affect events in a remarkable way.

What people think you expect of them, they will usually deliver. And what your own psyche, your own unconscious mind thinks you expect of it, it will deliver. When you hope strongly enough, expectancy goes to work for you. Great things happen.

I've gone through some difficult times—who hasn't?—and I know how easy it is to think that troubles have become your constant companions. You let a gray film of hopelessness creep into your mind, where it colors everything. You can even begin to enjoy this sense of hopelessness, in a perverse sort of way. It gives you an excuse for not trying to improve the situation!

The remedy for this state of mind is a good strong dose of hope, given to yourself at least three times a day. Don't ever say to yourself, "I've had it. I'm finished. I can't cope with all this." Never think, *This is more than I can take; it's more than I can handle.* Say aloud the words of the Psalm, "Hope thou in God: for I shall yet praise him" (42:11 KJV). ❧

*May your unfailing love rest upon us,
O LORD, even as we put our hope in you.*

— Psalm 33:22 NIV

❧

*A religious hope does not only bear up the mind
under her sufferings, but makes her rejoice in them.*

—Joseph Addison

54
Hope in God's Word

Richard Winter

Fresh light shall yet break out from God's Word.

—John Robinson

❧

The word "hope" is defined by the *Oxford Dictionary* as "desire joined with expectation of getting what is desired." We use the word with varying degrees of expectation of getting what we desire. I sense that in our culture it has become a very feeling-oriented word. "I hope that everything will work out all right" without much certainty that it will.

Perhaps our use of the word not only reflects a culture which lives more on feelings than facts, but also reflects the uncertainty of the world in which we live. The prophets of doom and gloom in the economic, social, and ecological disciplines, together with the daily news of wars and murders, have shattered our illusions of a happy future. Biblical writers, in contrast, used the word hope with the meaning of a strong desire joined with a deep conviction and expectation that what they desired would actually happen. Their hope was not based on speculation but on belief in God and what He had revealed about Himself. There were good reasons to believe.

What is the hope of which the biblical writers spoke so frequently? In the Old Testament we find Jeremiah reminding himself of God's character—that God is loving, faithful and just (Lamentations 3). Then we find David with hope in

God's Word: "I have put my hope in your word" (Psalm 119:74,81 NIV). In God's Word he found an explanation and the purpose of his life—where he had come from and where he was going to. He also knew that as he obeyed God's Word he would be living the way God intended him to live and so would be most fulfilled. God's Word also told him of salvation—of the promised Messiah and of life after death.

In the New Testament the same themes recur but in much more detail. Again and again the theme of hope is sounded in the context of encouragement in trial and difficulty. We are encouraged repeatedly to get our perspective right, to look up and beyond the trees. Paul in the middle of all his hardships and troubles says that he is "sorrowful, yet always rejoicing" (2 Corinthians 6:10 NIV).

In this broken world we will often experience two emotions at once, sadness at sin but at the same time rejoicing at what God is doing in us and in the world and at what He is going to do in the future. "Rejoicing" does not always mean happiness. It is an attitude of mind which may bring a feeling of happiness. As Martin Lloyd-Jones says, "Seek happiness and you will never find it. Seek righteousness and you will find you are happy." 🙐

You are my refuge and my shield;
I have put my hope in your word.

—Psalm 119.111 NIV

🙐

What can be hoped for which is not believed?

—Saint Augustine

55

Practicing Peace

Gien Karssen

Where there is peace, God is.

—George Herbert

❧

"May the Lord direct your hearts into God's love and Christ's perseverance. . . . Now may the Lord of peace himself give you peace at all times and in every way" (2 Thessalonians 3:5,16 NIV).

Each of Paul's thirteen letters begins with a greeting of peace. Some, like this one to the Christians in the Greek city of Thessalonica, end the same way.

These words were full of meaning. Paul was reminding the Thessalonians that the Lord, the author of peace, would give His peace always, in every way and under all circumstances. The Thessalonians needed this encouragement badly. They were people who suffered from oppression and persecution, who were confronted with the problem of immorality, who were full of sorrow because of loved ones who had died, who lived among difficult and pagan people, and who were confronted by false religious teachers and people with warped minds.

Paul's words referred back to the reality of the night in which Christ was born. The Lord Who gives peace, because He Himself is peace, was born to command peace. It is the same peace of which the Lord would later say to His disciples, "Peace I leave with you; my peace I give you" (John 14:27 NIV).

The Thessalonians claimed this peace, and proved it to be applicable and sufficient in their varied situations. This peace lifted them above their problems. In spite of pressure and adversity, their faith grew so that they became examples to others. Even today we can draw comfort from the experiences of those who have gone before us. We can try to follow their good example, learn not to lose heart, and nurture hope.

Circumstances today are far from rosy. The world finds itself in chaos. Many a family is in crisis. The church is often at a loss for the right answers. Small wonder that our hearts lack peace and are full of uncertainty. But in spite of this we can experience the Lord's peace continually, and in every way.

Peace must be practical and practiced! We best begin each day with God, reading His Word and praying. Then we can think back to this quiet time throughout the day to claim His peace when unrest and discord are knocking at our door. We must remind ourselves that no situation we find ourselves in is beyond the range of God's interest in us.

In this world you will have trouble. But take heart!
I have overcome the world.

—John 16:33 NIV

Speak, move, act in peace, as if you were in prayer.
In truth, this is prayer.

—Francois Fénelon

56

Choosing Joy

Luci Swindoll

Joy is the echo of God's life within us.

—Joseph Marmion

❧

I hadn't been on this earth very many years when it began to sink in that lots of things were not going to go my way. I'd get all excited about a plan or an event that was on the horizon of my life, when suddenly things didn't pan out and my spirit would hit rock bottom with a mighty thud. There was always a thief waiting in the wings to steal my joy and enthusiasm.

So much so that it finally struck me (sort of like being run over by a large truck), "How long are you going to live like this? How long are you going to let life sit on top of you with its disappointments, anxieties, pressures, and regrets? Why don't you figure out a way to beat life at its own game?"

That's when I decided to begin dwelling on the positive instead of the negative. That's when celebrating life became a conscious choice, a decision to live fully, every day and in every way, to the degree that I was able. That's when I realized that the presence of God could actually enter in my circumstances and change things for the better. And, oh, what a difference that change in attitude has made in the way I face life!

Believe it or not, we all have many reasons to celebrate life in spite of the situations in which we find ourselves. Today. This minute. There is something—some perk—in your life that is cause for celebration. Think about it. Start this way.

Look at the hour before you, with its myriad demands, plans, concerns and ask God, in the midst of all that, to give you a perk—just for the love of life . . . no other reason.

We all lead such busy, stressful lives. We feel overwhelmed. We experience pressure and nagging deadlines that drive us crazy. To celebrate anything for any reason would never enter our thinking. But believe me, we need those perks to keep going. They sweeten the bitter taste of life.

The highest and most desirable state of the soul is to praise God in celebration for being alive. Without perks our lives are easily lost in the world of money, machines, anxieties, or inertia. Our poor, splendid souls! How they fight for food! They have forgotten how to celebrate. They have forgotten how to request little perks.

Our hurried, stressful, busy lives are unquestionably the most dangerous enemy of celebrating life itself. Somehow, we must learn to achieve momentary slowdowns, and request from God heightened awareness of the conception that life is a happy thing, a festival to be enjoyed rather than a drudgery to be endured. Life is full of perks if we train our souls to perceive them.

Consciously, I believe we can be taught to do that. Celebrate everything under the sun. When we get into this mindset, living takes on a brand new feeling. There's praise instead of blame or complaint. Joy instead of sorrow. ❦

The joy of the LORD is your strength.

—Nehemiah 8:10 NIV

❦

Today well lived . . . makes every tomorrow a vision of hope.

—Anonymous

Everyday Miracles

Every believer is God's miracle.

—Philip James Bailey

57
Nothing Is Impossible

Dwight L. Moody

There is nothing which God cannot affect.

— Cicero

God likes His people to believe that there is nothing too hard for Him.

If you study the Bible, you will find out that no sooner did the news come up to heaven that Adam had fallen, than God was right down in Eden after him. Men sometimes get to be so big that they don't care for little things, but God never does. We are all the time limiting God's power by our own ideas. Let us get our eyes off one another and fix them upon God. There is nothing too hard for Him.

Whenever I go to a new place the people say, "Oh, yes, you did so and so in the city, but this place is very peculiar; there are special difficulties here such as you have never met before."

Yes, I suppose there are special difficulties in every case, but those obstacles won't stand in the way very long when God rises up to carry on His work. When Mr. Sankey and I first started out, we took Jeremiah 32:17 (KJV) for our motto: "Ah! Lord God . . . there is nothing too hard for thee," and we always had great success. After awhile we thought we would take some other motto, but we couldn't get on at all until we came back to this verse: "There is nothing too hard for thee."

Let us remember: "And of his fulness have all we received" (John 1:16 KJV). It is a very common fault with Christians to forget the Lord's fullness. They are living on stale manna, and trying to get happy over their past experience. They were converted twenty years ago, and they seem to think that the Lord gave them a blessing which was to last them all their lives. Not so. There is an infinite fullness in Christ, and those who believe in Him may receive of it all the time.

Ask Noah. He was able to live and preach 120 years, while he was about the only person in all the world who believed in God, and this he could do because he had received the Lord's fullness. Ask Abraham. He was able to offer up his only son at the command of God. Ask Joshua. He received the fullness, and nobody was able to stand before him all the days of his life.

There were the reformers Knox, Wesley, Whitefield, and Newton. Were they any greater men in intellect than a great many others in their time? By no means, but they received the Lord's fullness. That was what made them so great and strong in their work. Take the twelve apostles: they were not men of learning and science, they were not great orators, they were not rich, had no special position. But just think of a Galilean fisherman writing such a book as the Gospel of John! He had received the Lord's fullness. ⊛

Jesus looked at them and said, "With man this is impossible, but with God all things are possible."

—Matthew 19:26 NIV

⊛

If thou knowest God, thou knowest that everything is possible for God to do.

—Callimachus

58

The Meaning of Miracles

Calvin Miller

*God is a God of surprises. He makes walls
fall down, creates miracle children, and
causes water to gush forth from rocks.*

—Ruthann Ridley

Christ's birth was miraculous as was His resurrection. If we try to take away Christianity's miraculous heart, we destroy it.

Biblical miracles "set aside" nature for the welfare of people. This shows how much we mean to God.

Nature can be kind. When it is, we see God in the seagull's nest and the mountain stream. But what about when nature is not kind? What conclusions do we draw when quakes rip cities or villages are decimated with the plague? Do we say God is a fiend Who cares nothing for us?

Nature alone was not the way for God to say, "Man has a special meaning to me." But by suspending nature God could demonstrate that we mean more to Him than the created order.

Jesus ended Bartimaeus's blindness, and gave him sight by a supernatural act. The miracle proved that Bartimaeus was important to God. Jesus fed the five thousand because He had compassion on the hungry crowd. In considering such supernatural events we see our cosmic importance. Without a God Who gets involved in the natural world we are but unimportant microbes.

André Malraux has said, "The greatest mystery is not that we have been flung at random among the profusion of the earth and the galaxy of the stars, but that in this prison we can fashion images of ourselves sufficiently powerful to deny our nothingness." But he is only partly right. We would be nothing if we were not loved by God.

When we were children, the monsters of the dark seemed real and fanged, lurking in the hallway just outside our door. We heard the thunderous footfalls in the gloom. But they turned out to be only our father who heard us crying and came to comfort us. We never saw him in the darkness. But we felt his touch and knew he was there. The universe is vast and sometimes dark, but we are not alone. &

You are the God who performs miracles;
you display your power among the peoples.

—Psalm 77:14 NIV

&

To the true disciple a miracle only manifests the power
and love which are silently at work everywhere.

—Frederick William Robertson

59

Only Believe

Smith Wigglesworth

I believe because it is impossible.

—Tertullian

I love to sing that wonderful chorus, "Only Believe," because it is scriptural. It is from the words of Jesus to the synagogue ruler whose daughter had died. The chorus says:

> Only believe! Only believe!
> All things are possible,
> Only believe! Only believe!
> All things are possible,
> Only believe!

Our Lord Jesus says, "Only believe." He has ordained complete victory over difficulty, over every power of evil, over every depravity. Every sin is covered by Calvary.

Our Lord Jesus says, "All power is given unto me in heaven and in earth" (Matthew 28:18 KJV). He longs that we should be filled with faith and with the Holy Spirit, and declares to us, "He that believeth on me, the works that I do shall he do also; and greater works than these shall he do; because I go unto my Father" (John 14:12 KJV).

Jesus has gone to the Father. He sits in the place of power and He exercises His power not only in heaven, but on earth, for He has all power on earth as well as in heaven. What an open door to us if we will but believe Him!

The disciples were men after the flesh just like us. God sent them forth, joined to the Lord and identified with Him. Peter, John, and Thomas—how different they were! Impulsive Peter, ever ready to go forth without a stop. John, the beloved, leaning on the Master's breast. Thomas, with hard nature and defiant spirit, exclaimed, "Except I shall see in his hands the print of the nails, and put my finger into the print of the nails, and thrust my hand into his side, I will not believe" (John 20:25 KJV).

What strange flesh! How peculiar! But the Master could mold them. There was no touch like His. Under His touch even stonyhearted Thomas believed.

You may be ordinary, but God wants to make you extraordinary in the Holy Spirit. God is ready to touch and transform you right now.

It is God's intention to make you a new creation, with all the old things passed away and all things within you truly of God; to bring in a new, divine order, a perfect love, and an unlimited faith. Will you have it? ❧

Jesus told the synagogue ruler, "Don't be afraid; just believe."
— Mark 5:36 NIV

❧

Belief means that the truth has made a conquest in personality.
—Leslie D. Weatherhead

60

God Will Supply

Colleen Townsend Evans

Providence knows what we need better than we ourselves.

—Jean de La Fontaine

When it comes down to putting our needs into words, many of us falter. We feel selfish, greedy—yes, materialistic!—asking for such down-to-earth commodities as money, a place to live, a job, a car or access to dependable transportation, or training to make us more useful in the world. We don't want to bother God with such practical matters, so we keep these concerns to ourselves, reserving our prayers for things "more spiritual."

Yet there is the word *bread,* and what could be more down-to-earth than that? Surely, if Jesus meant for us to communicate with God only about spiritual matters, He would have used a different word. Bread is the simplest kind of food, the very staple of life from the beginning of recorded time. It has literally been the nutritional mainstay of civilization. And it is nourishment we need regularly, day by day, as Jesus also acknowledged by calling it "our *daily* bread."

[My husband Louie and I had many questions about asking for daily resources] when we began to explore petitionary prayer. We were in seminary, and had turned down a job with a regular paycheck so we could be free to do deputation work for the school. We were doing what we wanted to do, and what we felt God wanted us to do—so we were happy.

Then one day we had to face the fact that we had hardly any food left . . . and no money to buy more. Our need was specific, and real—so, putting our questions aside, we decided to take our need to God. I remember how uncomfortable we felt, kneeling and praying together for something as practical and unspiritual as our next meal. But we did it, believing that if God didn't approve of it, He would somehow let us know.

Later in the day, during a study break, Louie walked down the hill to our mailbox and brought back a letter from a church we had visited months before. As he opened it and read— "Sorry to be late—thanks, and God bless!"—a check for forty dollars fell to the floor. Forty dollars! We couldn't have been more thrilled if it had been 400. For it wasn't just money, it was an answer to a specific asking prayer—and for us, a new understanding of what it meant to pray for our daily bread.

I want to share something from *George Mueller, Man of Faith,* for I feel close to Mueller's concept of asking for specific needs, not from any selfish motive to glut myself on more and more things, but to be free to serve: "I first began to allow God to deal with me . . . and set out fifty years ago simply relying on Him for myself, family, taxes, traveling expenses, and every other need," he wrote. "I've lacked nothing—nothing!" &

And my God will meet all your needs according to his glorious riches in Christ Jesus.

—Philippians 4:19 NIV

I know no blessing so small as to be reasonably expected without prayer, nor any so great but may be attained by it.

—Robert South

61

The End of Ourselves

Keith Miller

Sin is energy in the wrong channel.

—Saint Augustine

☙

The way . . . surrender takes place may be different for each person, but certain events seem to "mark the trail" for almost everyone.

The universal nature of sin is such that without ever knowing it, all of us become centered in ourselves in a way that is not conducive to healthy relationships and to long-term happiness. We put ourselves in the center where only God belongs. The way this sin often manifests itself is that we gradually begin to focus on one thing in particular in our lives so much that eventually we cannot by our own strength want God more than that thing.

Since denial is operating, we don't see the extent to which our lives are being absorbed by whatever is capturing them (by promising to make us feel good or make us OK). Our attention can be captured this way by a chemical or other addictive substance, sex, gambling, or criminal habits. Or what we focus on can be something that is good in itself; it doesn't have to be a "bad" thing. For instance, this focus may be on a behavior, like work, or on another person, a mate, for instance, or a child, or it can be on religious programs or ourselves and our own ambitions. But whatever this unhealthy, compulsive attention is focused on, that is the controlling manifestation of our . . . particular sin.

Although we are not conscious that we are so intently focused on one area of our lives, the amount of time and attention we give that hottest area of our thoughts gives us away. And this thing that we put in the center of our living to satisfy us can become an idol, replacing God as the security and center of our lives.

As long as things are going well in the area of our sin-security, we feel important and in control. But sooner or later putting something or someone in the center of one's life, where only God belongs, leads a sensitive person to the end of his or her rope. Evidently nothing will give us the safety and power of God in our lives, except God.

When we . . . focus our lives upon anything or any relationship that is not God, sooner or later we spoil it, and it will fail us. For, in fact, we are not in control of life, and no thing or person can meet our deepest needs for security and fulfillment.

Throughout this process our sin tries to get us to deny that we are putting anything in God's place or that we are powerless to handle the situation. This is evidently because when we see and confess our sin we can repent, surrender, put God back in the center, and defeat the [sin] disease—thus overcoming the alienated, guilty feeling that things are not OK. And when God is in place in the center of our lives, then we have His power to confront and deal with the continuing insidious and addictive force of the [sin] disease. ❧

Then I acknowledged my sin to you and did not cover up my iniquity. I said, "I will confess my transgressions to the LORD"—and you forgave the guilt of my sin.

—Psalm 32:5 NIV

❧

As the earth can produce nothing unless it is fertilized by the sun, so we can do nothing without the grace of God.

—Vianney

62

You Can Change

Larry Crabb

Some things work suddenly and are seen; others,
such as the life of a seed, work slowly and silently.

—Oswald Chambers

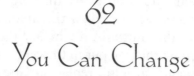

Perhaps the most confusing question that emerges from a study of change from the inside out is this: *How far inside do you have to look?* Once we agree an inside look is necessary for deep change, we enter the mouth of a dark cave that tunnels off in endless, uncharted directions.

Although an inside look can be overwhelming (and indeed must be if the core direction of our life is to really shift), still there must be more to it than a journey into darkness. We are children of light. Even in the midst of darkness, we know where we're headed. We have a lamp that always reveals the next step and a hope that keeps us moving even when the lamp seems to go out. Christians are not to be characterized by joyless confusion and morbid despair. And that's precisely what develops when we define the path to growth as an endless search for further awareness of all that's happening within us.

We must not mistake an intense, absorbing heaviness for spiritual depth. Spiritual depth frees us to be spontaneous in the midst of sadness. It enables us to press on in our involvement with people even when we stagger from blows of severe disappointment. A mature relationship with Christ is reflected in the capacity to hear whispers of assurance when discouragement is oppressive. And even when we're mishandling frustration by retreating to an angry pout, mature depth won't let us escape the convicting awareness that we're designed to love, even in *this* situation.

The purpose of an inside look is to promote that kind of spiritual depth. The more deeply we sense our thirst, the more passionately we'll pursue water. And the more clearly we recognize how we dig our own wells in search of water, the more fully we can repent of our self-sufficiency and turn to God in obedient trust. As we learn to live in confidence that the deepest concerns of our soul are in good hands, both the shame we feel because of our unworthiness and the terror we have of one day facing exposure and rejection will lose their power to control us. Change from the inside out involves a gradual shift away from self-protective relating to strongly loving involvement. And in order to make that change, we must feel our disappointment as a longing person and face the sin in our heart that results in a commitment to self-protection.

Change in the Christian life is progressive. We move from change in our conscious direction to change in our approach to relationships to change in the direction of our very being. Each change represents a work of God and is therefore good. New believers change in their conscious direction. Growing believers learn to love by abandoning their self-protection. Mature believers begin to grasp the meaning of Paul's words, "For me to live is Christ" (Philippians 1:21 KJV), as they shift the central direction of their very being toward God. ❧

I will give you a new heart and put a new spirit in you.
—Ezekiel 36:26 NIV

❧

Effective change happens with daily choices.
—Judith Couchman

63

The Second Lesson

Andrew Murray

The only important decision I have to make is
to live with God; He will make the rest.

—Anonymous

Following Christ in a holy life is impossible for people to do on their own. Alongside that is the thought, *What is impossible with men is possible with God.*

These thoughts mark the two great lessons we have to learn in the religious life. It often takes a long time to learn that first lesson—that in religion we can do nothing, that salvation is impossible to us. Often we learn that, yet do not learn the second lesson—that what has been impossible to us is possible with God. Blessed is the person who learns both lessons.

Your religious life is to be a living proof that God works impossibilities. Your religious life is to be a series of impossibilities made possible and actual by God's almighty power. That is what the Christian needs. He has an almighty God that he worships, and he must learn to say, "I do not want a little of God's power, but I want—with reverence be it said—that whole of God's omnipotence to keep me right and to live like a Christian."

The cause of the weakness of your Christian life is that you want to work it out partly, and to let God help you. That cannot be. You must come to be utterly helpless, to let God work—and God will work gloriously. I could go through

Scripture and prove to you how all God's servants in the Old Testament counted upon God's omnipotence on God doing impossibilities. And this God lives today; this God is the God of all His children.

Have you believed that Almighty God is able to reveal Christ in your heart so that the Holy Spirit rules in you, so that the self-life has no power or dominion over you? Have you, with tears of penitence and with deep humiliation and feebleness, cried out, "O God, it is impossible to me; man cannot do it; but, glory to Your name, it is possible with God"?

Have you claimed deliverance? Do it now. Surrender yourself afresh into the hands of a God of infinite love, and know that as infinite as His love, is His power to do it.

But he [God] said to me, "My grace is sufficient for you,
for my power is made perfect in weakness." Therefore
I will boast all the more gladly about my weaknesses,
so that Christ's power may rest on me "

—2 Corinthians 12:9 NIV

When I have realized my own helplessness and have
acknowledged it to Him, I have received some of
the greatest manifestations of His power.

—Kathryn Kuhlman

A Constant Help

Our loving Lord is not just present,
but nearer than thought can imagine.

—Amy Carmichael

64

A Very Present Help

Amy Carmichael

Without faith, we are as stained glass windows in the dark.

—Anonymous

Which is harder: to do or to endure?

I think to endure is much harder, and our Father loves us too much to let us pass through life without learning to endure. So I want you to welcome the difficult little things, the tiny pricks and ruffles that are sure to come almost every day. For they give you a chance to say "No" to yourself, and by doing so you will become strong not only to do but also to endure.

Whatever happens, don't feel sorry for yourselves. You know how our Lord met the tempting "Pity Thyself." After all, what is anything we have to bear in comparison with what our Lord bore for us?

I know that each one of you is in need of continual help if you are continually to conquer. I have splendid words to give you; they are from the first verse of Psalm 46 (KJV): "A very present help."

Our loving Lord is not just present, but nearer than thought can imagine—so near that a whisper can reach Him. You know the story of the man who had a quick temper and had no time to go away and pray for help. His habit was to send up a little telegraph prayer—"Thy sweetness, Lord!"—and sweetness came.

Do you need courage? "Thy courage, Lord!" Patience? "Thy patience, Lord!" Love? "Thy love, Lord!" A quiet mind? "Thy quietness, Lord!"

Shall we all practice this swift and simple way of prayer more and more? If we do, our Very Present Help will not disappoint us. For Thou, Lord, hast never failed them that seek Thee.

[Isaiah said,] "Thus spake Jehovah unto me like a firm grasp of the hand" (Isaiah 8:11). Sometimes this firm grasp comes through deepened insight into a single word. It has come to me through the word "trust," which I find in *Young's* means to *lean on—trust—confide*.

"I have trusted in Thy mercy [*leaned on* Thy mercy]" which has loved us with an everlasting love, which pardons and cleanses and will never tire of us. "He that trusteth in the LORD [*leaneth on* the Lord], mercy shall compass him about" (Psalm 32:10 KJV). Is it not like Him to let us know that He wants us to lean, not only on His mercy, but on His very Self?

"The LORD is my strength and my shield; my heart *leaned on* him, and I am helped: therefore my heart greatly rejoiceth; and with my song I will praise Him" (Psalm 28:7). &

God is our refuge and strength, an ever-present help in trouble

—Psalm 46:1 NIV

&

As sure as God puts His children into the furnace
of affliction, He will be with them in it.

—Charles Haddon Spurgeon

65

He Brings His Presence

Bob Benson

To abide increasingly in Christ is the portion of every believer.

—Andrew Murray

We can study and discuss what Jesus came to do for mankind. We can learn all the prophecies about Jesus and give our assent to them. They can even become our creeds and beliefs. But it is when we realize that He knows we do not have any bread, and that He is starting it down the table to us, that we suddenly know Who He is. He has been with us in our journey. He has been there all the time. He is with us.

Of course, there are reasons for believing in God. Theologians and thinkers have gathered them up for us and distilled them into a few classical arguments. The order and purpose of the universe certainly tells us that there must have been a Designer. And both the matter and the motion of the universe points to the conclusion that there was ultimately a first cause. And the very fact that always there have been men who have believed there was a God indicates there is One. Where else would the idea have come from? And we recognize evil because we somehow perceive the good, and those perceptions bring us to an absolute good or truth.

But to understand or repeat any of these beliefs or, indeed, all of them together, is not enough. When life caves in, you do not need reasons—you need comfort. You do not need some answers—you need someone. And Jesus does not come to us with an explanation—He comes to us with His presence.

We are always seeking the reasons. We want to know why. Like Job, we finally want God to tell us just what is going on. Why do the good die young and the bad seem to live on forever? If the meek inherit the earth, why do the arrogant always seem to have the mineral rights? But God does not reveal His plan—He reveals Himself.

> He comes to us in so many ways—
> Warmth when we are cold,
> Fellowship when we are alone,
> Strength when we are weak,
> Peace when we are troubled,
> Courage when we are afraid,
> Songs when we are sad,
> And bread when we are hungry.

He is with us on our journeys. He is there when we are home. He sits with us at our table. He knows about funerals and weddings and commencements and hospitals and jails and unemployment and labor and laughter and rest and tears. He knows because He is with us—He comes to us again and again—until we can say, "It's You! It's You!"

For Jesus came to be experienced. &

And surely I am with you always, to the very end of the age.
—Matthew 28:20 NIV

&

Whosoever walks toward God one cubit,
God runs toward him twain.
—Anonymous

66
Fear Not!

Lloyd Ogilvie

He who fears God need fear nothing else.

—Anonymous

The Lord takes hold of our right hand with His righteous, grace-filled right hand. That puts us eye to eye with Him. It's exactly what God intends. He has something He wants to say to us that He wants us to hear with the ears of our soul.

"You don't have to be afraid," He says. "I am in charge of your life. I will never leave or forsake you. Trust Me. Take the first step to living without fear. I am Jehovah-Shammah, the Lord is there. And wherever you are, be more sure of this than you are of your next breath—I will be there."

The Lord's constant word to us is "Fear Not!" There are 366 "Fear Not!" verses in the Bible—one for every day of the year and an extra one for Leap Year! Most of the admonitions are followed by a firm assurance of the Lord's presence or a stirring reminder of an aspect of His nature—like His faithfulness, goodness, lovingkindness, or intervening power in times of need.

Christ comes to you and me in our lonely fear with all power and authority. He will not leave us helpless in the restless seas of life.

Sometimes the Lord rides out the storm with us and other times He calms the restless sea around us. Most of all, He calms the storm inside us in our deepest inner soul. And when He does, we can begin to face all of the fears that disturb our thinking, in our personal relationships and responsibilities, and in our culture.

I experienced that peace when I first invited Christ to live in me in the spring of 1949. The following summer I went fishing in Canada with my dad. About that same time, he had renewed his faith in Christ. The Lord used our time to bind us into a deep relationship that we'd never known.

While we were fishing, a storm came up and thrashed the lake into dangerous waves. We were tossed about like a cork on the lake. Our small fishing boat was nearly capsized.

Then, when we thought all hope of surviving was gone, suddenly the wind subsided, and in a few minutes the lake was flat as a mirror.

Dad and I looked at each other. Then he said quietly, "Lloyd, the Lord is here!" And indeed He was.

But it no less convinced me that the Lord has been with me when the storms around me didn't cease. The sea He calms then is inside my soul. With that peace replacing our fears, we can take anything.

So fear not! You belong to the Lord and He will never abandon you. &

Fear not, for I have redeemed you;
I have summoned you by name; you are mine.

—Isaiah 43:1 NIV

&

Fear knocked at the door. Faith answered. No one was there.

—Anonymous

67

Happy in God's Presence

Charles Haddon Spurgeon

In my integrity you uphold me and set me in your presence forever.

—King David

How vividly the presence of God must have been realized by Christ at all times, for He was in the Father and the Father in Him.

We have been taught to see God around us in all things that exist, and in all events that happen; we are taught by the Spirit to recognize our Father's loving, all-pervading presence. Yet I know we do not discern it so constantly, clearly, and impressively as our Lord Jesus did. He looked upon the mountains, and sunlight on their brows was the smile of His Father. He saw the plains, and their harvests were His Father's bounty. To Him the waves of the sea were tossed in tempest by His Father's breath, or calmed by His Father's whisper. He fed the multitude, but it was with His Father's bread. He healed the sick, but the Father did the work. In all things about Him, He continually and distinctly recognized the active presence of the Most High.

Now, I pray our Lord to grant that by the blessed Spirit we may always be sensitive of the presence of God wherever we are. Is it not a sad proof of the alienation of our nature that though God is everywhere, we have to school ourselves to perceive Him anywhere? His are the beauties of nature, His the sunshine which is bringing on the harvest, His the waving grain which cheers the husbandmen, His the perfume which loads the air from multitudes of flowers, His the insects which glitter around us like living gems, and yet the Creator and Sustainer of all these is far too little perceived.

Refuse to see anything without seeing God in it. Regard the creatures as the mirror of the great Creator. Do not imagine that you have understood His works until you have felt the presence of the great worker Himself. Do not reckon that you know anything till you know that of God which lies within it, for that is the kernel which it contains.

Wake in the morning and recognize God in your chamber, for His goodness has drawn back the curtain of the night and taken from your eyelids the seal of sleep. Put on your garments and perceive the divine care which provides you with raiment from the herb of the field and the sheep of the fold. Go to the breakfast room and bless the God Whose bounty has again provided for you a table in the wilderness. Go out to business and feel God with you in all the engagements of the day. Perpetually remember that you are dwelling in His house when you are toiling for your bread or engaged in merchandise.

At length, after a well-spent day, go back to your family and see the Lord in each one of the members of it. At last, fall asleep at night as in the embraces of your God, or on your Savior's breast. This is happy living. ❧

Surely you have granted him eternal blessings and made him glad with the joy of your presence.

—Psalm 21:6 NIV

❧

We cannot get away from God, though we can ignore Him.

—William Allen Butler

68

The Need to Ask

John Fischer

The simple heart that freely asks in love, obtains.

—John Greenleaf Whittier

Asking is one of the hardest things we will ever do because it assumes a position of need. [Jesus tells us to ask of Him, but] most of us pass by this statement and never truly relate to it. We look at it like some kind of Santa Claus promise: We sit on Jesus' lap and ask for things (all of which we could do without) in a department-store culture full of nonessentials.

There's nothing deprecating about this kind of asking; because we fail to take the command to ask seriously, He never takes us seriously. Because we can't see this as more than a spiritual wish list, we dismiss the notion entirely. We don't ask because we don't seek to find out what Jesus desires in our asking.

Asking has nothing to do with sitting on Jesus' lap. Asking is a way of life with an open hand. To ask is to depend on someone other than yourself. It is very humbling. Asking indicates: I don't know. I failed. I ran out. I can't find it. I'm not sure. I don't understand. I forgot. I didn't listen. I didn't care. I was wrong. I'm not prepared. I need more information. I came up short.

There's an interesting dilemma here for Christians. If Christianity is no more than a system that answers all of life's questions, then to admit any of the above shortcomings is to be something less than a good Christian. But in our own attempts to be good Christians, we undermine our need for God. We want Christianity to work. We want it to exist in a closed system where every question has an answer, every problem has a solution. We want to show the world a neat, clean, open-and-shut case for Christianity. But in the process, we unknowingly shut out God.

Claiming to be wise, we become fools; we exchange the truth of God for a lie and worship the created things (our systems, principles, and formulas) rather than the Creator, Who is forever blessed.

That's why Jesus says we should ask. Asking puts us back on track with God. It assumes a need relationship with Him— a hand-to-mouth spiritual existence. A vulnerable daily dependence. In a society that rushes to fill every felt need, that steals away the soul of a person and offers to sell it back at a price, we need to rekindle what it means to ask God.

Ask, Jesus says. Ask. It's so simple—like a child. Ask. And when you receive, keep on asking. Don't accept a fake fill. Live in your thirst and you will live in Him. Open your hand. Ask. ❧

Until now you have not asked for anything in my name.
Ask and you will receive, and your joy will be complete.

John 16:24 NIV

❧

God is true; His promises are sure to those who seek.

—M. B. Plantz

69

The Help of Angels

Andrew Bandstra

Angels . . . are given to us as guardians.

— Saint Ambrose

When the heavenly duty roster came out, was one specific angel assigned to your personal care and security?

Some people believe that Acts 12:1-19 teaches this. Peter had been cast into prison by Herod. The church was meeting at the home of the mother of John Mark, praying for Peter's release. Meanwhile, an "angel of the Lord" came and miraculously extricated Peter from prison (though Peter thought he was seeing a vision).

Outside the prison, Peter became aware that an angel had rescued him from Herod's clutches. He went to the home of John Mark's mother and knocked at the outer entrance. Rhoda, the maid, came to answer the door and announced to the prayer group that Peter was outside. The church found Rhoda's announcement hard to believe. When Rhoda kept on insisting, they said, "It must be his angel" (Acts 12:15 NIV). They believed that every one had a personal guardian angel who might occasionally show himself in bodily form and who might resemble in appearance the person under his care. (Finally Peter was allowed to enter and to greet the astonished church.)

So it is possible there is a personal guardian angel assigned to each believer. On the other hand, this passage really only proves that some early Christians believed that to be the case. John Calvin, you may recall, said that we should say only that which is "true, sure, and profitable" about angels. And he raised the question of whether it is really "profitable" to believe in individually assigned guardian angels. He pointed out that if I am not satisfied by the fact that the whole heavenly host is watching out for me, then it is not clear what benefit I would derive from knowing that one angel has been assigned as my personal guardian.

Calvin may be right. Yet if belief that a particular angel has been assigned for your personal and perpetual security gives you the assurance of God's personal care of you, then I see no harm in holding to it. Just remember that it is really God's care through the angels that give us security.

One final word. The biblical teaching on God's care through guardian angels is not meant to make us careless or irresponsible. Do you remember when the devil quoted [Scripture] in the temptation of Jesus? He was encouraging Jesus to throw himself down from the pinnacle of the temple. Jesus responded with another text from Scripture: "It is written, 'Do not put the Lord your God to the test'" (Deuteronomy 6:16). &

For he will command his angels concerning you to guard you.

Psalm 91:11 NIV

&

An angel is a spiritual creature created by God . . .
for the service of Christendom and of the church.

—Martin Luther

70

Risky Living

Jamie Buckingham

It is only by risking . . . that we live at all.

—William James

We can be of good cheer because we have overcome the world.

This is what "risky living" is all about. A person can seek the kingdoms of this world or the kingdom of God. If he chooses this world he will go after things: houses, real estate, position, reputation, popularity, sensual gratification—all the things the world calls security. Or, he can seek the kingdom of God, risking everything on Jesus' promise to bring us into happiness and maturity.

To move into this realm of maturity calls for a total death to self. It means you are willing to be expendable, to give up all self-rights for the happiness of others. It means you submit yourself to the loving hand of God much as a pawn submits to a chessmaster: "In whatsoever square you choose to place me, there will I be content." So even if you are surrounded by knights, rooks, and bishops who desire to destroy you, you will raise your hands in praise and say, "Hallelujah! I'm expendable. I choose to give up my life for the glory of the King."

I have been encouraged by the story of William Carey, a young English shoe cobbler of the late eighteenth century. Carey believed God wanted him to carry the Gospel to the people of India. Carey's motto still excites people who dare to step out in faith: "Attempt great things for God. Expect great things from God."

The Christian takes his direction from a different King. He is not motivated by money, fear, or public opinion. Nor does he shrink just because his way is blocked by a mountain. He is like Thoreau's marcher, who hearing the sound of a different drummer, "steps to the music which he hears, however measured or far away."

The worst of all heresies is to despair of those childhood ideals, those dreams that stimulated us when our minds were still young. How many of us have reached the crisis of middle life and, disillusioned, put aside our resolves of faith because of the fantasies of fear?

Yet the most exciting people I know are those who leave the comforts and security of home, who turn their backs on well-paying jobs and worldly fame to go to the remote areas of the earth as missionary doctors, pilots, translators, and teachers. Many of them die on foreign soil, unrecognized by men. But the price of death is very small when compared to what they purchase by their risky living. After all, what's the use of living if you don't [with God's help] attempt the impossible? ✤

What good will it be for a man if he gains the whole world, yet forfeits his soul? Or what can a man give in exchange for his soul?

— Matthew 16:26 NIV

✤

The company of just and righteous men is better than wealth and a rich estate.

— Euripides

Living by Love

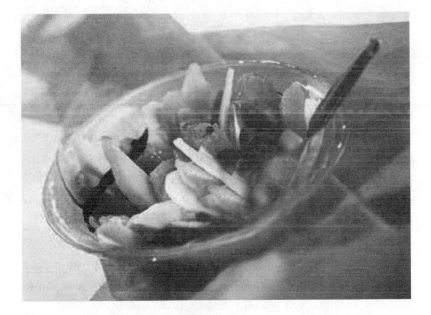

To love abundantly is to live abundantly.

—Anonymous

71

That We May Be One

John White

Lord, make me an instrument of Thy peace.

— Saint Francis of Assisi

It is not possible to exaggerate the importance of your fellowship with your fellow Christians. You need their love. You need their discipline. They need yours.

The Gospel was preached to you not primarily in order that you might be delivered from the torments of hell but that you might be brought into simultaneous fellowship with God and with your brothers and sisters. Such was the burden of Christ's priestly prayer in John 17.

The approach of death makes some men look into the future. Hours before His arrest and crucifixion, Jesus was pleading for the church of future ages. His vision encompassed you and me and the situations in which we, as Christians, find ourselves.

Curiously, He made only one request. He made other requests for the apostles; but when He addressed Himself to the church of the future, His requests were limited to one (John 17:20-23). He prayed only that we might be united, united not organizationally but in heart. "I in them and thou in me, that they may become perfectly one, so that the world may know that thou hast sent me and hast loved them even as thou hast loved me" (John 17:23 RSV).

The fact that He made only one request for the church of the future indicates the importance of what He asked for. Yet as we look at the nature of the request, we wonder why unity of spirit, important as it may be, should merit such exclusive attention.

He gives us a repeated clue to the puzzle. "That the world may believe" is the phrase He uses in verse 21 (NIV). For the church was to be left on earth for that purpose: that the world might believe. Power in testimony is evidently not something that the church can possess as a sort of separate package; it cannot exist alone. The church that convinces men that there is a God in heaven is a church that manifests what only a heavenly God can do, that is, to unite human beings in heavenly love. Wherever the sign of loving unity exists, the world will be convinced.

Miracles of healing, large mass rallies, power preaching, and super organization all may have their place. But there is nothing on earth which convinces people about heaven or that awakens their craving for it like the discovery of Christian brothers and sisters who love one another. ❧

My prayer is not for them alone. I pray also for those who will believe in me through their message, that all of them may be one, Father, just as you are in me and I am in you. May they also be in us so that the world may believe that you have sent me.

—John 17:20-21 NIV

❧

We are not sent into this world to do anything into which we cannot put in our hearts.

—John Ruskin

72

Looking for God's Messengers

Judith Couchman

Whenever we hear, we must listen.
"He who has ears to hear," Jesus says, "let him hear."

—John R. W. Stott

Looking for a messenger is as ancient as life itself. Since the Garden of Eden, humanity has hungered for meaning, wanting the way to redemption. We've yearned for someone to tell us the truth, to point us to the One greater than ourselves. In turn, God has answered our questions with Himself. Through prophets, poets, kings, and priests He has spoken to us. Even the beloved Son served as a messenger, only speaking what the Father told Him to say (John 8:28). The message was so sacred not even the Christ would add to or subtract from it.

Undoubtedly, salvation is God's most important message to us, but once we accept His forgiveness and new life, the messengers don't stop crossing our path.

It may surprise us, but to get our attention, He now and then communicates through nonbelievers. They might deliver a compliment, an off-handed remark, or an incisive barb that hands us God-inspired truth and insight. But frequently, it is our local Christian brothers and sisters who voice God's encouragement, correction, and guidance to us. The traveling evangelists and television preachers serve as conduits for God's messages, but most of hearing His voice occurs in up-close, ongoing relationships and community. This is what God intends for us.

When we join God's family, He calls us to the joys and tribulations of involvement. In true community, we give and take love, hope, guidance, inspiration, and encouragement, but we also bump into one another's doubts and disappointments, faults and frustrations, troubles and trepidations.

Not by accident, then, the Bible also emphasizes our need to forgive. If we travel full circle—speaking God's truth, making mistakes, and forgiving one another—we grow in grace, love, intimacy, security, and acceptance. And deep in our hearts, aren't these the gifts we want to receive?

As the Lord's followers, we're to assemble together, encourage others toward good works, rejoice and weep as a family, and bear one another's burdens. In effect, we are to be God's messengers to one another, depositing His hope and truth into hearts. I crave these relational bonds, but to create them, I need to accept their inherent human imperfections, including my own. I can't separate the delight from the difficulty.

However, when I think clearly about the facets of community, I admit that God's messengers to me have delivered many positive and encouraging words, which far outweigh the critical comments I've heard. They've echoed the Father's approval, compassion, and creativity. This, too, is what God intends for us all. ⚬

See, I will send my messenger, who will prepare the way before me.

—Malachi 3:1 NIV

⚬

When we believe that God lovingly seeks our best and that
He is vastly more sensitive to us than we are to ourselves,
we will seek to hear Him.

—Martha Thatcher

73

Tough Love Lasts

James Hilt

Suffering is the true cement of love.

—Paul Sabatier

Have you ever felt compelled to show love in some tangible way, only to end up clutching inside? You felt a strong impulse to help another person or group. And you were about to take the plunge when something deep down inside of you cried out, "Don't do it! You could get hurt. Better play it safe."

Often our love is restricted by our fear of getting hurt. We dread being vulnerable. We have seen people in great need. But, committed to self-preservation, many people do not extend help to them. Instead of helping, they use rationalizations to justify their indifference: "That person wouldn't be thankful for anything I could possibly do. So why try?" Or, "There's so much suffering in the world. My puny efforts wouldn't even make a dent."

Who, in your mind, provides the best example in history of one who avoided emotional shelters, who best exhibited vulnerable love? Undoubtedly, the best example is Christ. If ever a person had an opportunity to shelter Himself, it was He. Safety was found in heaven. And refusing to cross into dangerous territory, He could have stayed there.

But, instead, Christ chose to become flesh, to plunge into a world torn apart by conflict and despair. Determined to flesh out His love, Christ became a man. But, while He did so, His foreknowledge told Him that He would bear, more than any other man, the pain of this world. Allowing Himself to be clothed with a human body—including a nervous system—Christ foreknew that excruciating pain would come from blows to His face by burly Roman soldiers, a crown of thorns on His head, and burning spikes in His hands and feet. By setting foot on this planet, Christ knew that Satan and his legions of darkness would take every opportunity to try to crush Him. He would experience unprecedented spiritual warfare, culminating in a hideous death on the cross.

But, hungry to reconcile, Christ met physical and spiritual horrors head-on. He courageously faced immeasurable sufferings, so that we might be transferred from the domain of darkness to the domain of His marvelous light.

Christ's love was committed, enduring, and tough! His love was not weak and wavering, but strong and persistent. And it is His full intent that our love become durable like His. ❧

For I am convinced that neither death nor life, neither
angels nor demons, neither the present nor the future,
nor any powers, neither height nor depth, nor
anything else in all creation, will be able to separate us
from the love of God that is in Christ Jesus our Lord.

—Romans 8:38-39 NIV

❧

God's love is not a conditional love; it is an open-hearted,
generous, self-giving love which God offers to [us].

—J. B. Phillips

74

Forgiving Others

Charles Stanley

Those who forgive most, shall be most forgiven.

—Josiah W. Bailey

[To forgive,] we must recognize that we have been totally forgiven. Most people get hung up on this point. Paul sums up [our foundation for forgiveness] beautifully: "For the death that He died, He died to sin once for all; but the life that He lives, He lives to God" (Romans 6:10 NKJV).

Once we understand the depth of our sin and the distance it put between us and God and once we get a glimpse of the sacrifice God made to restore fellowship with us, we should not hesitate to get involved in the process of forgiveness. To understand what God did for us and then to refuse to forgive those who have wronged us is to be like the wicked, ungrateful slave Jesus described in Matthew 18:23-34 (NIV).

Therefore, the kingdom of heaven is like a king who wanted to settle accounts with his servants. As he began the settlement, a man who owed him ten thousand talents was brought to him. Since he was not able to pay, the master ordered that he and his wife and his children and all that he had be sold to repay the debt.

The servant fell on his knees before him. "Be patient with me," he begged, "and I will pay back everything." The servant's master took pity on him, canceled the debt and let him go.

But when that servant went out, he found one of his fellow servants who owed him a hundred denarii. He grabbed him and began to choke him. "Pay back what you owe me!" he demanded.

His fellow servant fell to his knees and begged him, "Be patient with me, and I will pay you back." But he refused. Instead, he went off and had the man thrown into prison until he could pay the debt.

When the other servants saw what had happened, they were greatly distressed and went and told their master everything that had happened.

Then the master called the servant in. "You wicked servant," he said, "I canceled all that debt of yours because you begged me to. Shouldn't you have had mercy on your fellow servant just as I had on you?"

In anger his master turned him over to the jailers to be tortured, until he should pay back all he owed.

We read the parable and think, *How could anyone be so ungrateful?* But the believer who will not forgive another is even more guilty and more ungrateful than that slave. We have been totally forgiven of a debt we could never repay and thus have no grounds for refusing to forgive others. &

Forgive, and you will be forgiven.

—Luke 6.37 NIV

&

If God loved you as much as you love Him, where would you be?

—Anonymous

75

A Cup of Cold Water

Dietrich Bonhoeffer

*Give what you have. To someone it may be
better than you dare to think.*

— Henry Wadsworth Longfellow

"And whosoever shall give to drink unto one of these little ones a cup of cold water only in the name of a disciple, verily I say unto you, he shall in no wise lose his reward" (Matthew 10:42 KJV).

The bearers of Jesus' word receive a final word of promise for their work. They are now Christ's fellow-workers, and will be like Him in all things. Thus they are to meet those to whom they are sent as if they were Christ Himself.

When they are welcomed into a house, Christ enters with them. They are bearers of His presence. They bring with them the most precious gift in the world, the gift of Jesus Christ. And with Him they bring God the Father, and that means indeed forgiveness and salvation, life and bliss. That is the reward and fruit of their toil and suffering.

Every service we render then is service to Christ Himself. This means grace for the church and grace for the disciple in equal measure. The church will be readier to give them its service and honor, for with them the Lord Himself had entered into their midst. But the disciples are given to understand that when they enter into a house they do not enter in vain. They bring with them an incomparable gift.

It is a law of the kingdom of God that every person shall participate in the gift which we willingly receive as a gift from God. The man who receives a prophet and knows what he is doing will participate in the prophet's cause, his gift, and his reward. He who receives a righteous man will receive the reward of a righteous man, for he has become a partner in His righteousness. He who offers a cup of cold water to the weakest and poorest who bears no honorable name has ministered to Christ Himself, and Jesus Christ will be His reward.

Thus the disciples are bidden lastly to think, not about their own way, their own suffering, and their own reward, but of the goal of their labors, which is the salvation of the church.*

Give, and it will be given to you. A good measure, pressed down, shaken together and running over, will be poured into your lap. For with the measure you use, it will be measured to you.

—Luke 6:38 NIV

God gives us two hands—one to receive with and one to give with. We are not cisterns made for hoarding; we are channels made for sharing.

—Billy Graham

* Reprinted with the permission of Simon & Schuster from *The Cost of Discipleship* by Dietrich Bonhoeffer. Translated from the German by R. H. Fuller with some revision by Irmgard Booth. Copyright © 1959 by SCM Press, Ltd.

76

Loving People I Don't Like

Jerry White

*The difference between duty and love is that the
first represents Sinai and the second represents Calvary.*

— Richard Braunstein

A part of living under the lordship of Christ is allowing unlovable people into our lives, people who we would never choose on our own. They enter our lives, often like a storm, disturbing our tranquility and testing our patience.

Paul gives us some guidelines for dealing with these people: "Now we who are strong ought to bear the weaknesses of those without strength and not just please ourselves. Each of us is to please his neighbor for his good, to his edification. Therefore, accept one another, just as Christ also accepted us to the glory of God" (Romans 15:1-2,7 NASB).

The first requisite for loving the unlovable is to realize how Christ accepted you. Where would you be today without Him? What if His acceptance had been conditional? Realize that right now Christ fully accepts you as you are, full of imperfections and problems, all of which He knows completely.

The second emerges from a basic decision to accept everyone God brings across your path. In God's plan there are no accidental meetings. In each encounter God has a purpose for both the needy person and you. You may be the one who can really help and counsel the person.

Determine to be an encouragement to everyone whom God brings across your path. It costs little to say a kind word and to communicate a sense of support. But like the girl who doesn't want to encourage a suitor, we fear that kind words will lead to further demands. Such is the risk.

[I need to remember that] through the years others have so graciously put up with my pestering personality. During my early days of [ministry], I knew I was abrasive and demanding. Many of my friends graciously ignored these signs, helping me to grow. Even today, I know I can irritate people of a particular personality type, yet they accept me.

I appreciate the instruction of Hebrews 13: "Keep on loving each other as brothers. Do not forget to entertain strangers, for by so doing some people have entertained angels without knowing it. Remember those in prison as if you were their fellow prisoners, and those who are mistreated as if you yourselves were suffering" (Hebrews 13:1-3 NIV).

We never know where a kindness will lead, because only God can see the potential of the man or woman in our presence. &

Now that you have purified yourselves by obeying
the truth so that you have sincere love for your brothers,
love one another deeply, from the heart.

—1 Peter 1:22 NIV

God's love for poor sinners is very wonderful, but
God's patience with ill-natured saints is a deeper mystery.

—Henry Drummond

77

The First Fruit of the Spirit

Dwight L. Moody

True Christianity is love in action.

—David O. McKay

≈

The fruit of the Spirit is love. What a heavenly grace love is! It has its center in the heart, but its circumference sweeps, like omnipresence, around everything. Love is a grace of boundless scope. We love God. It is the only way in which we can embrace Him fully. We love His dear Son as He is. We love the ever-blessed Spirit as He is.

Following upon this, for God's sake we love the creatures He has made. Every tiny fly is sacred to our souls as God's creature. Our love climbs to heaven, sits among the angels and bows among them in lowliest attitude, but in due time our love stoops to earth, visits the haunts of depravity, cheers the garrets of poverty, and sanctifies the dens of blasphemy, for it loves the lost. Love knows no outcast; it has cast out none. It talks not of the "lapsed masses," for none have lapsed from its regard. Love hopes good for all, and plans good for all. While it can soar to glory it can descend to sorrow.

Love is a grace connected to eternity, for we shall never cease to love Him who first loved us. But love has also to do with this present world, for it is at home in feeding the hungry, clothing the naked, nursing the sick, and liberating the slave. Love delights in visiting the fatherless and the widows, and thus it earns the encomium, "I was an hungered, and ye gave me meat: I was thirsty, and ye gave me drink: I was a stranger, and ye came unto me" (Matthew 25:35).

Love has to do with friends and family. How fondly it nestles in the parental bosom! How sweetly it smiles from a mother's eye! How closely it binds two souls together in marriage bonds! How closely it walks along the ways of life, leaning on the arm of friendship! But love is not content with this. She embraces her enemy; she heaps coals of fire upon her adversary's head; she prays for them that despitefully use her and persecute her. Is not this a precious jewel indeed? What earthly thing can be compared to it?

In the list of the fruit of the Spirit, love is the first. It is first because in some respects it is best. First, because it leads the way. First, because it becomes the motive and stimulant of every other grace and virtue.

Love fulfills the whole law. You cannot say that of any other virtue. Yet, while it fulfills the law, it is not legalistic.

Love, moreover, is Godlike, for God is love. Love prepares us for heaven, where everything is love. Come, sweet Spirit, and rest upon us till our nature is transformed into the divine nature by our burning flames of love. Oh, that it were so with us this very day! ❧

A new command I give you: Love one another. As I have loved you, so you must love one another. By this all men will know that you are my disciples, if you love one another.

—John 13:34-35 NIV

❧

These Christians love each other even before they are acquainted.

—Saint Celsus

Eternal Promises

The created world is but a small parenthesis in eternity.

— Sir Thomas Browne

78

Our Final Destiny

Sinclair B. Ferguson

*Heaven will be the endless portion of every man
who has heaven in his soul.*

—Henry Ward Beecher

God encourages us in the long, slow process of transformation to full [spiritual] sonship. He has predestined us to be conformed to the image of His Son! Christ has prayed that we may share in His glory! Not only so, but the ultimate reason for our salvation and spiritual transformation further guarantees that we will successfully pass through the dangers and trials of the Christian life. For God's purpose is that Christ should be the firstborn in an innumerable company of brothers!

There is rich blessing and encouragement for us in our salvation, but it is all for God's glory and for the pleasure of His Son, Jesus Christ. Since in Christ we are more than conquerors (Romans 8:37), we can receive the promise that Christ Himself has given: "To him who overcomes, I will give the right to sit with me on my throne, just as I overcame and sat down with my Father on his throne" (Revelation 3:21 NIV). Then the blessings of the covenant that God makes with all His sons will be fulfilled: "He who overcomes will inherit all this, and I will be his God and he will be my son" (Revelation 21:7 NIV).

At last, the Father and son will be fully and finally united in eternal fellowship! We will share in the regeneration of all things toward which the whole creation moves under the sovereign direction of God the Father. In the meantime, as God's children, we are being . . .

Changed from glory into glory,
Till in heaven we take our place,
Till we cast our crowns before thee,
Lost in wonder, love, and praise.

—*Charles Wesley*

Then, we who now enjoy the liberty of the grace of God, will enjoy forever the liberty of the glory of the children of God (Romans 8:21). For "now we are children of God, and what we will be has not yet been made known. But we know that when he appears, we shall be like him, for we shall see him as he is" (1 John 3:2 NIV).

Do you now think of your relationship to God in terms of a son with his loving, forgiving Father? Or do you still think of yourself as the Father's "hired servant" (Luke 15:19)? ❧

In all these things we are more than conquerors through him who loved us.

—Romans 8:37 NIV

❧

In heaven, to be even the least is a great thing, where all will be great; for all shall be called the children of God.

—Thomas á Kempis

79

Satisfied with Life

Peter E. Gillquist

No man is living at his best who is not living at his best spiritually.

—W. Marshall Craig

The Bible says, "Be strong in the Lord and in the strength of His might" (Ephesians 6:10 RSV). And my heart says, "That's the way I want to be." It's not that I want power to step all over people and get my way, but I do want to know by experience that dominion which I was created to possess. As a new Christian I needed security; today I wish to live in His power and say with Paul, "I have strength for every situation through Him who empowers me" (Philippians 4:13).

There will come a day when I need neither security nor power. In the New Jerusalem those two will have slipped on by, for there I shall know honor and glory. And that is just what He has promised! That is what the whole business of rewards is all about—God bestowing His honor upon us.

The psalmist records, "I will . . . honor him. I will satisfy him with a long life and show him my salvation" (Psalm 91:15-16). When you see the end of things, you can go through virtually anything to get there. When I see what God has prepared for those who love Him, everything along the way seems hardly worthwhile taking that into account.

Regardless of the circumstances now, God promises us honor, satisfaction, salvation! Can you think of any way to improve that? No wonder Paul had the courage to say, "For I am convinced that neither death nor life, neither angels or authorities, neither present nor future affairs, neither power of the heights nor of the depth, nor anything else created will be able to separate us from the love of God that is in Christ Jesus our Lord" (Romans 8:38-39). What else really counts?

Besides honor, He promises satisfaction for the length of our lives. Wow! As a nonbeliever I used to sweat death and wonder what on earth I could do with my life to make it significant. Now earth life is not the issue. A friend in Memphis said to me recently, "The more I grow in the Lord, the more I see that physical death is not all that big a deal." God says whatever the length of our lives, we will be satisfied with what He gives us, for real life never ends.

When troubles used to come, I would always try to analyze "why." That doesn't get it any more. I don't care why. I am learning, slowly, that what happens to me is God's business. He is working it together for good; He asks me to simply thank Him and see that because of what is ahead my head should be there instead of only here! ❧

My soul will be satisfied as with the richest of foods;
with singing lips my mouth will praise you.

—Psalm 63:5 NIV

❧

The truest end of life is to know that life that never ends.

—William Penn

80
Celebrating Life

Henri Nouwen

The great use of life is to spend it for something that outlasts it.

—William James

When we speak about celebration we tend rather easily to bring to mind happy, pleasant festivities in which we can forget for a while the hardships of life and immerse ourselves in an atmosphere of music, dance, drinks, laughter, and a lot of cozy small-talk.

But celebration in the Christian sense has very little to do with this. Celebration is possible only through the deep realization that life and death are never found completely separate. Celebration can really come about only where fear and love, joy and sorrow, tears and smiles can exist together. Celebration is the acceptance of life in a constantly increasing awareness of its preciousness. And life is precious not only because it can be seen, touched, and tasted, but also because it will be gone one day.

When we celebrate a wedding we celebrate a union as well as a departure; when we celebrate death we celebrate lost friendships as well as gained liberty. There can be tears after weddings and smiles after funerals. We can indeed make our sorrows, just as much as our joys, a part of our celebration of life in the deep realization that life and death are not opponents but do, in fact, kiss each other at every moment of our existence.

When we are born we become free to breathe on our own but lose the safety of our mother's body; when we go to school we are free to join a great society but lose a particular place in our family; when we marry we find a new partner but lose the special tie we had with our parents; when we find work we win our independence by making our own money but lose the stimulation of teachers and fellow students; when we receive children we discover a new world but lose much of our freedom to move; when we are promoted we become more important in the eyes of others but lose the chance to take many risks; when we retire we finally have the chance to do what we want but lose the support of being wanted.

When we have been able to celebrate life in all these decisive moments where gaining and losing—that is, risking life and death—touch each other all the time, we will be able to celebrate even our own dying because we have learned from life that those who lose it can find it. &

For whoever wants to save his life will lose it,
but whoever loses his life for me will find it.

—Matthew 16:25 NIV

&

Make sure the thing you're living for is worth dying for.

—Charles Mayes

81

Keeping Our Sights on Heaven

Mother M. Angelica

He who thinks most of heaven will do most for earth.

—Anonymous

When you ask me, "What will heaven be like?" I must answer that it will be more perfect than any of us could say. Whatever your best concept of total happiness is, it's nothing compared to heaven.

In heaven we won't need the things that are so necessary in this life. When we die, we will bring only ourselves, our souls, and our love. We will stand alone before God. At that moment, God will become our "all." We will have no need for worldly comforts, for there will be no voids, no needs. Our attachment will be to God alone. Once God becomes our "all," we will have everlasting and sublime joy. We will be totally content. And we will lack nothing.

As we move forward on our spiritual journey, we realize that heaven is not an invention of the mind: it is the goal of our souls. It is not a payoff for being good, but a vision we long to see. Heaven is a state and place. It is the extraordinary gift of God. You and I will never, in this life, be able to comprehend what heaven looks like or feels like, to know, to imagine whether the music will be harpsichord, or flute, or the awesome silence of God's loving face, our mental pictures of the robes and the gardens and the clouds and the winged angels may be inadequate, but they're not foolish.

They are merely the most we can do with the tiny glimpses of light we have received.

Heaven may seem difficult to understand, and that's okay. It's not easy to comprehend a place where everything is perfect, where sin cannot reign, where God is visibly present to us always. But we can never let the confines of our mind thwart our pursuit of the truth. Logic will give us a start on the matter, but only faith, hope, and love can fill our minds with ideas and truths we could not otherwise grasp. If you pray to God for understanding, He will give it to you. If you say to Him, "Lord, help me to know what is true," you will come to know more than you ever imagined possible.

"Ask and you shall receive." You will be amazed at the light and insight God will give you, if only you will ask. You will realize that your confusion, your questions, and your skepticism all have a purpose: to bring you closer to God.

See you in heaven! &

He will swallow up death forever.
The Sovereign LORD will wipe away the tears from all faces.

—Isaiah 25:8 NIV

&

If the way to heaven be narrow, it is not long;
and if the gate be straight, it opens into endless life.

—William Beveridge

82

Treasures in Heaven

Dwight L. Moody

Our heart is in heaven, our home is not here.

—Reginald Heber

≫

If we are living as the Lord would have us live, our treasures are laid up in heaven, and not laid up on the earth. I think we would be saved a great many painful hours, and a great deal of trouble, if we would just obey this portion of Scripture, and lay up our treasures in heaven. It is just as much a command to lay up our treasures in heaven, and not upon the earth, as it is a command not to steal.

It doesn't take long to tell where a person's treasure is. It doesn't take long to find out where a person's heart is. You talk with a person five minutes, and if he has his heart upon one object, you will find out. And if you want to find out where a person's treasure is, it won't take long to find that out, either. The Bible tells us, "Where your treasure is, there shall your heart be also."

The reason we have so many earthly minded people and so few people with heavenly minds is because many have their whole hearts set upon earthly pleasures and objects, and few have their treasures laid up in heaven. If your treasure is here, you will be disappointed and in trouble and trial, when the Lord has told you plainly to lay up your treasures in heaven, where moth and rust do not corrupt, nor thieves break through and steal.

Now, here is the command: "Lay not up for yourselves treasures on earth, but lay up for yourselves treasures in heaven."

Where is your treasure? In other words, where is your heart?

In Hebrews 11:13-14 (KJV), there are these words: "These all died in faith, not having received the promises, but having seen them afar off, and were persuaded of them, and embraced them, and confessed that they were strangers and pilgrims on the earth. For they that say such things declare plainly that they seek a country." Then in the tenth verse of the same chapter, speaking of Abraham, it says, "For he looked for a city which hath foundations, whose builder and maker is God" (KJV).

The moment Abraham caught sight of that city, he proclaimed himself a pilgrim and a stranger. The well-watered plains of Sodom had no temptation for him. He declared that he saw another country—a better country. He had turned his heart from this fleeting world, and Sodom with all its temptations didn't tempt him. He had something better. How poor a man is, no matter how much he has laid up in this world, if he has not his treasure laid up on heaven! ❧

The kingdom of heaven is like treasure hidden in a field.
When a man found it, he hid it again, and then in his joy
went and sold all he had and bought that field.

—Matthew 13:44 NIV

❧

I should not give one moment of heaven for
all the joy and riches of the world, even if it
lasted for thousands and thousands of years.

—Martin Luther

83

A Glimpse of Paradise

Ann Spangler

Heaven's the perfection of all that can be said or thought.

—James Shirley

Then the angel showed me the river of the water of life, as clear as crystal, flowing from the throne of God and of the Lamb down the middle of the great street of the city. On each side of the river stood the tree of life, bearing twelve crops of fruit, yielding its fruit every month. And the leaves of the tree are for the healing of the nations.

No longer will there be any curse. The throne of God and of the Lamb will be in the city, and his servants will serve him. They will see his face, and his name will be on their foreheads. There will be no more night. They will not need the light of a lamp or the light of the sun, for the Lord God will give them light. And they will reign for ever and ever" (Revelation 22:1-5 NIV).

Chapters 21 and 22 in the Book of Revelation are some of the most beautiful and comforting in all of Scripture. Finally, the blood, the smoke, and the terrible destruction of this apocalyptic vision are drawing to a close. Evil has been utterly destroyed and God is wiping away every last tear from every last eye. Death and mourning and crying are words now relegated to an archaic dictionary. The night is gone and darkness has vanished.

This, at last, is the world we have dreamed of all our lives. A world in which love prevails and sorrow is forever banished. A world in which we never misunderstand and are never misunderstood. We have come home to a land of ecstasy, where we will see God face to face for an eternity of days.

Even with the help of Revelation, Paradise is hard to contemplate. How can we possibly imagine a world we have never even glimpsed? Perhaps we envision heaven as the cessation of our sufferings. But this is only a negative vision—the relief we feel from the absence of pain. Who among us can imagine what it will be like to be constantly encircled by joy?

It is only too easy to forget about Paradise in the world we live in. But if we open our eyes, we may yet catch a glimpse of it. Why not take a moment to reflect on these two chapters of Revelation? Let God show you the kind of eternity He has prepared for you. Remember that you were made not just for this world, but for the world that is to come. ❧

Jesus answered him, "I tell you the truth,
today you will be with me in paradise."

—Luke 23:43 NIV

❧

Joy, joy for ever!—my task is done—
The gates are pass'd, and heaven is won!

—Sir Thomas Moore

84

The Glory Ahead

Billy Graham

Heaven is the presence of God.

—Christina Georgina Rossetti

I believe we are living in the most challenging generation in history. As the world rushes headlong toward Armageddon, our attention should be centered on telling everyone about the One Who is waiting to give us relief from this suffering world.

In the Bible God gives us a glimpse of what heaven will be like for believers. It will have the characteristics of a happy home, a holy city, a glorious garden, and a beautiful bride. This staggers the imagination!

God has prepared a place that will give us relief from suffering and renewed vitality for serving the Savior. An unknown devotional writer has said:

Heaven is a place of complete victory and triumph. *This* is the battlefield; *there* is the triumphal procession. *This* is the land of the sword and spear; *that* is the land of the wreath and crown. Oh, what a thrill of joy shall shoot through the hearts of all the blessed when their conquests shall be complete in heaven, when death itself, the last of foes, shall be slain—when Satan shall be dragged captive at the chariot wheels of Christ—when He shall have overthrown sin—when the great shout of universal victory shall rise from the heart of all the redeemed.

Ahead of us is the triumphal procession—the glorious victory and reality of heaven. Some day we will see "a new heaven and a new earth, the home of righteousness" (2 Peter 3:13 NIV). Some day "the trumpet will sound, the dead will be raised imperishable, and we will be changed" (1 Corinthians 15:52 NIV). Some day we will receive "an inheritance that can never perish, spoil or fade—kept in heaven for you" (1 Peter 1:4 NIV). Some day "when he appears, we shall be like him, for we shall be like him, for we shall see him as he is" (1 John 3:2 NIV). Someday the suffering and the pain of this world will be over, and we will be with God forever in heaven.

Until that glorious day—till Armageddon—let us live for Christ. Let us trust Him. Let us turn to Him in our time of need. And let us joyfully walk hand in hand with our Lord Jesus Christ—regardless of our circumstances—until we personally and physically join Him throughout eternity! &

I consider that our present sufferings are not worth comparing with the glory that will be revealed in us.

—Romans 8:18 NIV

&

Earth has no sorrow that heaven cannot heal.

—Sir Thomas Moore

Credits

The following excerpts were used by permission of their respective copyright holders. Other works are in public domain.

1. John R. W. Stott, *Basic Christianity*. © 1971 Inter-Varsity Press, London. Used by permission of the Wm. B. Eerdmans Publishing Co. and Inter-Varsity Press, London.
2. A. W. Tozer, *The Root of the Righteous*. © 1955 Christian Publications, Inc. Used by permission.
3. *Lessons from a Sheep Dog*, Philip Keller. © 1983, Word Publishing, Nashville, Tennessee. All rights reserved.
4. Excerpted from the book, *Designing a Woman's Life*, by Judith Couchman, Multnomah Publishers, Inc. © 1995 by Judy C. Couchman. Used by permission.
6. Excerpt (submitted) from *The Magnificent Defeat* by Frederick Buechner. © 1966 by Frederick Buechner. Copyright © renewed 1994 by Frederick Buechner. Reprinted by permission of HarperCollins Publishers, Inc.
7. From *The One Year Book of Quiet Times with God* by Jill Briscoe. © 1997. Used by permission of Tyndale House Publishers, Inc. All rights reserved.
8. Hannah Whitall Smith, *Daily Devotions from the Christian's Secret of a Happy Life* (Grand Rapids, MI: Fleming H. Revell, a division of Baker Book House Company. 1984), 87, 89.
9. Edith Schaeffer, *A Way of Seeing*, published by Fleming H. Revell, a division of Baker Book House. © 1977. Used by permission.
10. *Biblical Ethics* by Oswald Chambers. © 1947 by the Oswald Chambers Publications Assn. Ltd., and is used by permission of Discovery House Publishers, Box 3566, Grand Rapids, MI 49501. All rights reserved.
11. "Open-Hearted Bible Study" by Jean Fleming. First published in *Discipleship Journal*. © Jean Fleming. Used by permission of the author.
12. Excerpted from the book, *Lord, Heal My Hurts,* by Kay Arthur; Multnomah Publishers, Inc. © 1989 by Kay Arthur. Used by permission.
14. Calvin Miller, *The Taste of Joy*. © 1983. Used by permission of the author.
15. Excerpted from the book, *The Signature of Jesus,* by Brennan Manning; Multnomah Publishers, Inc. © 1992 by Brennan Manning. Used by permission.
16. Jeanne Guyon, *Experiencing the Depths of Jesus Christ*. © 1975 by The SeedSowers, Box 285, Sargent, GA 30275. Used by permission.
17. Excerpt (submitted) from *Prayer: Finding the Heart's True Home* by Richard J. Foster. © 1992 by Richard Foster. Reprinted by permission of HarperCollins Publishers, Inc.
19. From the article, "Soul Talk," by Gordon MacDonald, originally printed in *Discipleship Journal*, Issue 88, 1994. Used by permission of the author.
20. Peter Marshall, *The Best of Peter Marshall*. Published by Chosen Books, Inc., a division of Baker Book House Company. © 1977. Used by permission.

21. Taken from *Daring to Draw Near* by John White. © 1977 InterVarsity Christian Fellowship/USA. Used by permission of InterVarsity Press, P. O. Box 1400, Downers Grove, IL 60515. Also used by permission of Inter Varsity Press, London.

22. Catherine Marshall, *Beyond Ourselves*. Published by Chosen Books, Inc., a division of Baker Book House Company. © 1961. Used by permission.

23. Excerpted from *God Is Great, God Is Good* by Michael Griffiths. © 1987 by Michael Griffiths. Published by NavPress. Originally published in the United Kingdom by Hodder and Stoughton as *Down to Earth God*. Used by permission of the author.

24. From *The Unselfishness of God* by Hannah Whitall Smith. © 1987 Littlebrook Publishing, Inc., Princeton, NJ 08540. Used by permission.

25. Eugene H. Peterson, *Traveling Light*. © 1988 by Eugene H. Peterson. Published by Helmers and Howard Publishers, Inc. Used by permission.

26. Excerpted from *Mere Christianity* by C. S. Lewis. © 1952. Used by permission of HarperCollins Publishers Ltd., London.

27. From *Ever Increasing Faith* by Smith Wigglesworth. © 1971 by Gospel Publishing House, Springfield, MO. Used by permission of Gospel Publishing House.

28. Taken from *How to Give Away Your Faith* by Paul E. Little. © 1988 by Marie Little, revised edition. Used by permission of InterVarsity Press, P. O. Box 1400, Downers Grove, IL 60515.

29. Excerpted from the book, *No Wonder They Call Him the Savior,* by Max Lucado; Multnomah Publishers, Inc. © 1986 by Max Lucado. Used by permission.

30. Reprinted from *Bold Love*. © 1992 by Dan Allender and Tremper Longman III. Used by permission of NavPress, Colorado Springs, CO. All rights reserved. For copies call (800) 366-7788.

31. Reprinted from *Transforming Grace*. © 1991 by Jerry Bridges. Used by permission of NavPress, Colorado Springs, CO. All rights reserved. For copies call (800) 366-7788.

32. Taken from *In His Image* by Paul Brand and Philip Yancey. © 1984 by Paul Brand and Philip Yancey. Used by permission of Zondervan Publishing House.

33. Taken from *Growing Strong in the Seasons of Life* by Charles Swindoll. © 1983 by Charles R. Swindoll, Inc. Used by permission of Zondervan Publishing House.

34. Taken from *Loving God* by Charles Colson. © 1983, 1987 by Charles W. Colson. Used by permission of Zondervan Publishing House.

35. *Facing Reality* by Oswald Chambers. © 1939 by the Oswald Chambers Publications Assn. Ltd., and is used by permission of Discovery House Publishers, Box 3566, Grand Rapids, MI 49501. All rights reserved.

36. Taken from *Women of Character* by Debra Evans. © 1996 by Debra Evans. Used by permission of Zondervan Publishing House.

37. From *The Normal Christian Life* by Watchman Nee. © 1957 by Angus I. Kinnear. First published by Gospel Literature Service, India. American

edition published in 1977 by Tyndale House Publishers, Inc. Used by permission of Kingsway Publications, Ltd., Sussex, England. All rights reserved.

38. Taken from *The Adversary* by Mark I. Bubeck. © 1975, Moody Bible Institute of Chicago. Moody Press. Used by permission.

39. *Transforming the Daily Grind* by Stuart Briscoe. © 1995. Used by permission of Harold Shaw Publishers, Wheaton, IL 60189.

40. From *A Woman's Guide to Spiritual Warfare.* © 1991 by Quin Sherrer and Ruthanne Garlock. Published by Servant Publications, Box 8617, Ann Arbor, Michigan, 48107. Used by permission.

42. Taken from *Ordinary Women, Extraordinary Strength* by Barbara Cook. © 1988 by Barbara Cook. Used by permission of the author and Peacemakers Ministries, Inc., Australia.

43. Excerpt (submitted) from *The Adventures of Living* by Paul Tournier. © 1965 by Paul Tournier. Reprinted by permission of HarperCollins Publishers, Inc.

44. Taken from *Fearfully and Wonderfully Made* by Paul Brand and Philip Yancey. © 1980 by Paul Brand and Philip Yancey. Used by permission of Zondervan Publishing House.

45. Pat Robertson, *My Prayer for You,* published by Fleming H. Revell, a division of Baker Book House Company. © 1977. Used by permission.

46. Reprinted from *The Freedom of Obedience* by Martha Thatcher. © 1986 by Martha Thatcher (Nav Press, 1986), 84-87. Used by permission of the author.

47. Elisabeth Elliot, *Discipline: The Glad Surrender.* Published by Fleming H. Revell, a division of Baker Book House Company. © 1982. Used by permission.

48. Excerpt (submitted) from *The Confident Woman* by Ingrid Trobisch. © 1993 by Ingrid Trobisch. Reprinted by permission of HarperCollins Publishers, Inc.

49. Corrie ten Boom, *Plenty for Everyone.* Published by Fleming H. Revell, a division of Baker Book House Company. © 1967. Used by permission.

50. Taken from *Diamonds in the Dust* by Joni Eareckson Tada. © 1993 by Joni Eareckson Tada. Used by permission of Zondervan Publishing House.

51. Reprinted from *God by Moonlight* by Amy Carmichael, © by Christian Literature Crusade. Used by permission.

52. Robert A. Schuller, *Power to Grow Beyond Yourself.* Published by Fleming H. Revell, a division of Baker Book House Company. © 1987. Used by permission.

53. Norman Vincent Peale, *Power of the Plus Factor.* Published by Fleming H. Revell, a division of Baker Book House Company. © 1987. Used by permission.

54. Reprinted from *The Roots of Sorrow* by Richard Winter. © 1986 by Richard Winter. Used by permission of the author.

55. Reprinted from *Beside Still Waters* by Gien Karssen. © by Gien Karssen. Used by permission of the author.

56. Reprinted from *Celebrating Life*. © 1989 by Luci Swindoll. Used by permission of NavPress, Colorado Springs, CO. All rights reserved. For copies call (800) 366-7788.

58. Calvin Miller, *A Hunger for Meaning*. © 1984. Used by permission of the author.

59. From *The Anointing of His Spirit*. © 1994 by Wayne Warner. Published with Servant Publications, P. O. Box 8617, Ann Arbor, Michigan, 48107. Used with permission.

60. From *Give Us This Day Our Daily Bread* by Colleen Townsend Evans. © 1981 by Colleen Townsend Evans and Laura Hobe. Used by permission of Doubleday, a division of Bantam Doubleday Dell Publishing Group, Inc.

61. Excerpt (submitted) from *Sin: Overcoming the Ultimate Deadly Addiction* (PB Title: *Hope In the Fast Lane*) by J. Keith Miller. © 1987 by John Keith Miller. Reprinted by permission of HarperCollins Publishers, Inc.

62. Reprinted from *Inside Out*. © 1988 by Dr. Lawrence Crabb. Used by permission of NavPress, Colorado Springs, CO. All rights reserved. For copies call (800) 366-7788.

64. Reprinted from *Candles in the Dark* by Amy Carmichael. © 1981 by Christian Literature Crusade. Used by permission.

65. Reprinted from *In Quest of the Shared Life* by Bob Benson. © Bob Benson, 1986. Generoux Publishers, 3900 Plantation Drive, Hermitage, Tennessee, 37076.

66. Reprinted from *Fearless* by Lloyd Ogilvie, to be released in 1999. © 1999 by Lloyd Ogilvie. Used by permission of the author and Andrew Lawler Company.

68. *True Believers Don't Ask Why* by John Fischer, Bethany House Publishers. © 1989 by John Fischer. Used by permission.

69. From *In the Company of Angels* © 1995 by CRC Publications. 2850 Kalamazoo SE, Grand Rapids, Michigan 49560. Copublished with Servant Publications, P. O. Box 8617, Ann Arbor, Michigan, 48107. Used by permission.

70. Reprinted from *Risky Living* by Jamie Buckingham. © 1976 by Jamie Buckingham. Used by permission of the author.

71. Taken from *The Fight* by John White. © 1976 InterVarsity Christian Fellowship/USA. Used by permission of InterVarsity Press. P. O. Box 1400, Downers Grove, IL 60515.

72. Excerpted from the book, *His Gentle Voice,* by Judith Couchman, Multnomah Publishers, Inc., copyright 1998, by Judy C. Couchman. Used by permission.

73. Reprinted from *How to Have a Better Relationship with Anybody* by James Hilt. © 1984 by James Hilt. Used by permission of the author.

74. Reprinted from *Forgiveness* by Charles Stanley. Published by Thomas Nelson Publishers. © 1987 by Charles Stanley. Used by permission.

75. Reprinted with the permission of Simon & Schuster from *The Cost of Discipleship* by Dietrich Bonhoeffer. Translated from the German by R. H. Fuller with some revision by Irmgard Booth. © 1959 by SCM Press, Ltd.

About the Compiler

Judith Couchman is the owner of Judith & Company and works full-time as an author and speaker. She is the author/compiler of twenty-three books, including *A Garden's Promise, His Gentle Voice, The Woman Behind the Mirror, Shaping a Woman's Soul* and *Designing a*  *Woman's Life*. Before starting her own company, she was the founding editor-in-chief of *Clarity*, a national magazine for Christian and spiritually seeking women.

With more than twenty years in the publishing industry, Judith has served as director of product development for NavPress periodicals, director of communications for The Navigators, editor of *Sunday Digest* and managing editor of *Christian Life*. She has worked as a public relations practitioner, a freelance reporter and a high school journalism teacher. In addition, she has earned an M.A. in journalism and a B.S. in education.

Judith has received national awards for her work in religious publishing, corporate communications, and secondary education, and speaks to women's and professional groups around the country. She lives in Colorado.

For additional information or to contact the author, you may visit her website at:

www.judithcouchman.com

Additional copies of this book and other titles by
Judith Couchman are available from your local bookstore.

If you have enjoyed this book, or if it has impacted
your life, we would like to hear from you.

Please contact us at:

RiverOak Publishing
Department E
P. O. Box 700143
Tulsa, Oklahoma 74170-0143

www.riveroakpublishing.com